W9-CLY-497

3 2109 00031 8973

WITHDRAWN
University Libraries
University of Memphis

A Doubleday Anchor Book $2.50

Serge Chermayeff **Christopher Alexander**

COMMUNITYANDPRIVACY

Toward a New Architecture of Humanism

JOHN BRISTER LIBRARY
MEMPHIS STATE UNIV
MEMPHIS, TENN. 38152

Serge Chermayeff, architect and planning consultant, was born in Russia and studied architecture and art in England and on the Continent before coming to the United States during World War II. He was chairman of the Department of Design, Brooklyn College; President of the Institute of Design, Chicago; lecturer at M.I.T., and professor at the Graduate School of Design at Harvard. He is now Professor at Yale.

He has been in architectural practice in England, California, New York, and Boston, and in addition to planning and designing public and private buildings has designed furnishings, special interiors, and fixtures, and has been essayist, lecturer, and critic in England and the United States. He is a fellow of both the Royal Institute of British Architects and the Royal Society of Arts.

Christopher Alexander was born in Vienna and educated in England. He received his B.A. in architecture and his M.A. in mathematics from Trinity College, Cambridge, and his Ph.D. in architecture from Harvard University. He is a fellow of the Society of Fellows of Harvard University. A British subject now living in the United States, Mr. Alexander teaches in the Department of Architecture at the University of California, Berkeley.

Serge Chermayeff Christopher Alexander

Chermayeff, Sergius Ivan

Toward a New Architecture of Humanism

COMMUNITYANDPRIVACY

Anchor Books   Doubleday & Company, Inc.   Garden City   New York

Community and Privacy was originally published
by Doubleday & Company, Inc., in 1963.

Anchor Books edition: 1965
ISBN: 0-385-03476-8
Copyright 1963 by Serge Chermayeff
All rights reserved
Printed in the United States of America
9 8 7 6

copy 3

To Walter Gropius
with admiration
affection and gratitude

NA
9031
C5
1965
Copy 3

Acknowledgments

This book was made possible by a grant to the authors from the Joint Center for Urban Studies of M.I.T. and Harvard. Particular thanks are due to Professor Martin Meyerson, the Director, for his continuing encouragement and help, and to collaborators John Meunier, Alden Christie, and Robert Reynolds, students at the Harvard Graduate School of Design, whose patience, energy, and skill in design, research, and in drawing produced the final comparative material and plans. Also to Miss Mac-Namara, the librarian at the Graduate School of Design, and Miss Kauffman, reference librarian, for their help in finding the required source material; to the Computation Center at M.I.T., which allowed us the free use of the IBM 704 to make the analysis of our problem; to Saul Steinberg for generously allowing the reproduction of his penetrating cartoons; to Elizabeth Bartlett Gordon, patient in editing and retyping the first draft; to Anne Freedgood, who gave logic and shape to what we wrongly believed to be the final draft; last but not least to Peter Chermayeff, who helped at every stage of the work and finally designed the illustrations, layout, typography, and jacket of the book.

SC CA, Cape Cod, 1962

Contents

The summary of a report on population growth by Heinz von Foerster is quoted by permission of the author. The quotation from Marshall McLuhan's letter of December 19, 1960, from Toronto is reprinted with the permission of Marshall McLuhan. The four drawings by Saul Steinberg are reprinted by permission of Saul Steinberg. The segmented circular diagram of three magnets: town, country and suburb is reprinted from Ebenezer Howard, *Garden Cities of Tomorrow,* London: Faber & Faber, Ltd., 1946, by permission of the publisher. The development cycle diagram from K. Lönberg-Holm and C. Theodore Larson, *Development Index,* Ann Arbor, The University of Michigan Press, 1953, is reprinted by permission of the publisher. The drawing of Orrubio Nuraghe, the fortress d'Orrolli, Nuoro, Sardinia, by Giovanni Lilliu, is reprinted with permission; copyright©1959 by *Scientific American,* Inc.; all rights reserved. The plan of the Baphoun temple is reprinted by permission of B. P. Groslier, E.F.E.O.—Conservation d'Anghor. The diagram describing the interaction of technology, obsolescence and design, by Frederick J. Kiesler, is reprinted from Frederick J. Kiesler, "On Correalism and Biotechnique," *Architectural Record,* September, 1939; copyright 1939 by F. W. Dodge Corporation with all rights reserved; reprinted by permission of the publisher and of Frederick J. Kiesler. The Schematic diagram of the process of abstracting, by A. Korzybski and Wendell Johnson, is reprinted from Wendell Johnson, *People in Quandaries,* New York: Harper & Row, Inc., 1946, by permission of the publisher.

Illustrations

Foreword

Every month enough human beings to make a city the size of Detroit are added to the world's population. In a few years it will be a city the size of Chicago every single month.

We are all aware of the population explosion, although with our present economy of abundance and our still uncrowded country, we are, most of us, only intellectually aware of it. And very few of us are aware of how rapidly its effects are being felt in many parts of the world. It is a pity that we all can't travel in time and space and visit Madras and Canton and Java in 1850, and 1900, and today. Those of us who are old enough can at least compare life in our own cities, in Paris and London and New York, a generation ago and now.

Man creates his own environment—and at an accelerated pace. Create is hardly the word, so far as he has simply made it, in the sense we say, "Well, you've made your bed, now you'll have to lie in it." It is obvious that it is on the verge, even in the richest and most highly developed countries, of getting beyond him. Today, in the words of Frank Lloyd Wright, it is easier to get someplace crawling over the tops of New York taxi cabs than inside one.

Most speculation about the dangers of the population explosion are concerned with economic factors—especially with the dwindling food supply and the exhaustion of natural resources. There is another, graver danger, the aesthetic danger. This may sound frivolous to some, but indeed it is not. On the organic, physiological, neurological, emotional, response of man to his environment depends his health as a species.

We make fun of the word "togetherness" but there is nothing funny about the increasing failure of our own togetherness with ourselves and the rest of life on this planet.

13

Ecology is the science of the togetherness of living things and their environment. Man is so radically altering the ecological situation out of which he emerged as a species, and altering it in such an irrational manner, that he is endangering his own future. If, in the next century the world grows to five billion people (and at present rates it will grow to far more than that) all living in a hundred thousand or more Calcuttas and Harlems, it may be possible to feed everybody on tanks of algae in the cities, the farming of the sea, the synthesization of foodstuffs from minerals, and the growing of vast mountains of living meat in reservoirs of culture media, but something will have happened to the human species. If it survives under such conditions it will certainly survive only by beginning to turn into another kind of animal, and, from our point of view at least, not a very nice kind. We talk of the waning of the humanist tradition. It is specific humanness itself which is threatened. Montaigne or Sophocles could not flourish in present-day Jakarta. What are the beings that will be the fittest to survive when such communities have spread over the surface of the earth?

The probabilities are that man will discover ways to limit population during the next generation. Or perhaps the too probable nuclear war will solve the problem out of hand and reduce the population to a few millions in the Tropics and the Southern Hemisphere. Meanwhile the inchoate spread of inhumane communities goes on. Urban renewal, what the French call urbanisme, suburbia, exurbia—aseptic slums proliferate.

We all remember the aquarium in our high school biology class, where the colony of Volvox grew over in one corner, in the spot of optimum light and temperature. Man is altering, as it were, the temperature and light and salinity of his own aquarium, irrationally, and with no knowledge of the possible results. Nobody knows what may happen.

Nature makes man. Man makes culture. Culture makes man. Man destroys nature. Consider the ecologically stable environment out of which man as a species probably developed. It must have been something like the climax formation of the eastern United States, a vast deciduous forest broken by parklands—only probably somewhat warmer. Where is that forest now? Does the present man-made environment of the eastern United States bear any resemblance to it? How much of this kind of change can we stand? It is already greater than the ecological changes that set in in the late Jurassic period and doomed the giant reptiles.

Archaeologists and cultural anthropologists and of course economists often talk of culture as though it were just a mass of pots and arrowheads, ruined buildings, kinships, initiation ceremonies, food crops, value, price and profit—things and their relationships, sweeping inexorably through time, with no self-conscious chunks of human vitality around at all. Are we just vehicles for the evolution of our artifacts—which will eventually overwhelm and exterminate us?

This is the role of the architect, the landscape architect, the community planners—the creative reconstruction of our ecology. Today we have the knowledge and the techniques. It is perfectly possible to rebuild deliberately the human environment, in such a way that the ultimate result will be the widening and deepening of the life of the species as such, the augmenting increase of life scope, aesthetic enrichment in the most profound sense. This, I suppose, is the only kind of "creative evolution" of which we are capable. But it is possible that we are capable of that.

This is the purpose of a book such as this. What the authors are talking about is much more than the efficient organization of the shelter of a community. At least their discussion is posited on an unusually profound sense of the meaning of the word "efficient." The ideal community structure—the actual fabric of buildings and land—should be like a culture medium, like the optimum part of the tank where the Volvox flourished, a culture medium that stimulates and enriches, like a circumambient food, the creative responses of the community to its most human life.

We have a long tradition of community planning of this sort. We have a great deal of rather general or philosophical discussion. Geddes and Mumford are names known to every educated layman. But I know of few works that approach the problem so directly in terms of the actual physical structuring. What do we need for a biological optimum? How do we define these needs in terms of cubic feet of filled and empty spaces?

The bias of this book may be ecological, but it is a human ecology. The authors are well aware that new factors operate that are not important to the balance of life in a tide pool, or the optimum growth of chaparral on a dry hillside. A large share of man's activities are social, but they ultimately, however practical and outgoing, have their source in privacy. Man is not only a rational animal, he is a contemplative one. We think of contemplation as a religious exercise, as prayer in church or monastery, or perhaps as quiet meditation in a park or garden. But the basic unit of human activity for most people, and for society as a whole, is the family. It is precisely the private familial peace, what might be called the inner life of parents and children, that our communities seem built to corrode and disrupt. Family prayers are long since out of date, but there is a kind of secret family ingathering of strength which is essential to human life. Above all other things, it is this that it is Serge Chermayeff's main concern to enable, protect, and enrich.

It would be easy to call this book a sort of exercise in human biotechnical engineering. It certainly is that, and masterfully so. It seems to me it is more than that. It is an exercise in creative or constructive humanism, but in a special sense. The guide here is such a work as Werner Jaeger's *Paideia*. We are to think in terms of a kind of higher hygiene—the planned ambiance of the most abundant life.

What good will it all do? Can we possibly stop the avalanche of our own insensate constructions? I don't know. There are so many negative factors operating against the survival, let alone the evolution, of the species, that the outlook is gloomy indeed. However, a book like this is a powerful force in the other direction. Who knows what single flicker of cosmic radiation once altered a gene somewhere back in geologic time and made all the difference? Certainly this one book is a small but potent dose of creative evolution. Enough like it and the vast tides of our own biological history may, just may, turn.

Kenneth Rexroth

Since this book was published in September 1963, many comments have been received and have suggested the notes for new readers which follow. These are intended as guides for the interested layman or professional who wishes to follow the whole argument, rather than defend his "Establishment."

The conflicts between private freedom and public responsibility are becoming sharper in all human affairs. The search to resolve these conflicts must include all those engaged in the design of man's environment, and must be understood by all those who commission their designs.

Since this book was first conceived several years ago some threatening pressures have been recognized outside the design profession: the growth in population and the pollution by man of his environment have received wide publicity. Much has been written on the mixed blessings of the car and the problems of traffic in towns. Man's increasing mobility is continuously encouraged, but a complementary tranquillity is seldom thought about.

The formidable problems created by electronics, the revolution in communications systems, in education, in employment, and leisure remain, for all intent and purpose, unrecognized by designers.

Two recurring reactions of readers deserve special comment. First, the book is not about "court houses," except incidentally. This ancient urban dwelling type does, however, provide, with appropriate rearrangement, a viable form of family dwelling on the ground in crowded places even to this day. Second, this book does not advocate the substitution of computer techniques for human thought. It simply recognizes the usefulness of this new tool in the design process and provides an example of its application to a familiar situation where it produces a surprisingly different solution.

The technical process is necessarily simplified for this book's purposes. The professional reader wanting to learn more of this is referred to *Some Notes on the Synthesis of Form* by Christopher Alexander, published in the summer of 1964 by the Harvard Press.

To summarize the authors' intention: the book advocates the development of a Science of Environmental Design to supplement high purpose, creative ability, and technical skill before it is too late; "Beauty will look after herself," to quote Eric Gill.

Serge Chermayeff
Cape Cod   June 1964

PART I: MASS CULTURE

ART & MASS CULTURE

BACKGROUND

We are now passing through a period of transition in the state of man quite as large and as far reaching as the transition from pre-civilized to civilized society. I call this the transition from civilization to post-civilization. This idea is shocking to many people who still think what is going on in the world today is a simple extension of the movement from pre-civilized to civilized society. In fact, however, we have to recognize that we are moving towards a state of man which is as different from civilization as civilization itself was from the pre-civilized societies which preceded it. This is what we mean by the innocent term "economic development." There is something ironic in the reflection that just at the moment when civilization has, in effect, extended itself over the whole world and when pre-civilized societies exist only in rapidly declining pockets, post-civilization is stalking on the heels of civilization itself and is creating the same kind of disruption and disturbance in civilized societies that civilization produces in pre-civilized societies.

Professor Kenneth E. Boulding

Conference on the City in History

Harvard, 1961

Cities were always a means of achieving some degree of simultaneity of association and awareness among men. What the family and the tribe had done in this respect for a few, the city did for many. Our technology now removes all city walls and pretexts.

The oral and acoustic space of tribal cultures had never met visual reconstruction of the past. All experience and all past lives were *now*. Preliterate man knew only simultaneity. The walls between men, and between arts and sciences, were built on the written or visually arrested word.

With the return to simultaneity we enter the tribal and acoustic world once more. Globally.

Marshall McLuhan

The Media Fit the Battle of Jericho

Explorations Six, July 1956

As for the idea of a disseminated urban culture linked by TV channels, I can only say I don't believe it probable and hope it is impossible. I have done a great deal of radio and TV cross talk and it is never satisfactory. For one thing, you cannot do what Mr. Dean Acheson has recently reminded us is often desirable, namely take a poke at your interlocutor. No, there are many things that must be done, face to face, not as in TV, "person to person." The reproduction of the human race is one of them and another is the using of the city for its highest purposes, the civilization of mankind.

D. W. Brogan
Conference on the City in History
Harvard, 1961

In place of the imminent values that arose, in the incipient stages of their development, out of the primal instincts, man will come to depend, under this new dispensation, upon increasingly rational and wholly extrinsic solutions of his problems. In short, a new manner of approach in the very perception and appraisement of phenomena, social no less than natural, is fashioning the world. How far we are justified in attempting to establish the consequences of this trend in shaping the edifice of the future, it would be difficult to say; certainly our own contemporary judgment of its essential character will in all probability not be shared by those destined to inhabit it. For the individual of the future will indubitably be as different from us in his basic orientation to life as his society and his world are certain to be different from ours. And though he will of necessity be more fully integrated and profoundly ad-

justed to his world than we, living in a transitional era, are to ours, we dare hardly peer beyond this generalization in our attempt to portray him. For our efforts in this direction will doubtless prove even more questionable and difficult, more arbitrary and unrewarding, than our attempts to comprehend the mental and emotional responses of our remote ancestors in prehistoric times.

Roderick Seidenberg
Posthistoric Man, 1957

The effects produced with the help of our contraptions (for example, the killing of millions of people with one hydrogen bomb) are so great, that we are no longer in a position to comprehend them. The links between intent, deed and effect are broken.

Max Born
Bulletin of the Atomic Scientists
June 1960

As man proceeds toward his announced goal of the conquest of nature, he is writing a depressing record of destruction—destruction of the earth he inhabits and destruction of the life that shares it with him. The history of recent centuries has its black passages—the slaughter of the buffalo on the Western plains, the massacre of the shore birds by the market gunners, the near extermination of the egrets for their plumage. Now to these, and others like them, we are adding a new chapter—the killing of birds, mammmals, fishes, and, indeed, every form of wildlife by chemical insecticides indiscriminately sprayed on the land.

Rachel Carson
Silent Spring, 1962

Progress in technology . . . has a tendency to grow as each invention and improvement facilitates the next step. But as long as fluctuations predominate, caused by the accidents of politics, by war and economic strife, this growth will not be apparent. Such was the case until about 1600. Then the rise began, which became rapid from about 1800 on, and is breath-taking today. It will continue so, if a catastrophe does not put an end to everything.

Max Born
Bulletin of the Atomic Scientists
June 1960

But if [man, "the paragon of animals"] allows himself to multiply unchecked, he is in danger of becoming *the planet's cancer.* After all, what is a cancer? It is a monstrous, or pathological, growth whose cells have ceased to be con-

trolled in their proliferation, have embarked on a course of unlimited multiplication, and have lost some or all of their organization.

Julian Huxley
Man's Challenge: The Use of the Earth
Horizon, September 1958

The growth of a population of replicating elements is said to be stable, if at all times the number of elements is finite. Populations of independent elements, e.g., yeast cells in an abundant nutrient, or populations of interacting elements competing for limited commodities, e.g., animals in a fixed ecology, are examples of populations with growth stability. While in the former case the growth of the population is characterized by a doubling time that remains constant, in the latter case it is the number of elements that remains constant.

The growth of a population is said to be unstable, if at a given instant of time the number of elements increases beyond all bounds. This is, for instance the case if the elements are capable of forming coalition, i.e., if two elements jointly can achieve more than these elements could ever achieve separately. Expressed in exact mathematical language, the growth of such an unstable population is given by

$$N = K / t^{k}$$

where N stands for the number of elements at any instant of time, K and k are characteristic constants, and t is the "countdown" in years, with "time zero" being the instant of instability, i.e., where the population annihilates itself by overpopulation $(N - x)$.

Clearly man with his capacity to communicate belongs in the category of coalition-forming elements and, hence, the growth of the human population follows the above equation. Using well established estimates of the world population of the last ten millennia, one calculates for the characteristic constants K = 180 billions, k = 0.98 and for the "time zero" to fall into the year A.D. 2027. In other words, it is in 65 years, or within a life span, that the human condition as we know it today is threatened with extinction.

One of the dramatic consequences of this growth mechanism is the steady decline of the doubling time (DT) of the human population. This is roughly indicated in the following expression;

$$DT = \frac{1}{2} t$$

where t is again the countdown in years. Consequently, at the time of Christ (t = 2027) it took the human population about 1000 years, at the turn of the first millennium (1 = 1027), about 500 years to increase to twice its size. At the turn of our century we observe the world population to double as quickly as 62 years and in about 33 years from today we will see our cities swollen up to twice their present size to accommodate a population that has multiplied by two in just one generation.

Heinz von Foerster

Summary of report on population growth, 1962

Each individual uses the store of randomness, with which he was born, to build during his life rules which are useful and can be passed on. Similarly, we can detect in the process of evolution the increasing randomness of all living things. The higher animals, in a sense, are more different from their surroundings than are the lower. We might therefore take as our general picture of the universe a system of continuity in which there are two elements, randomness and organization, disorder and order, if you like, alternating with each other in such a fashion as to maintain continuity.

John Zachary Young
Reith Lectures, 1950
Doubt and Certainty in Science, 1951

In our everyday life we experience not solid and immediate facts but stereotypes of meaning. We are aware of much more than what we have ourselves experienced, and our experience itself is always indirect and always guided. The first rule for understanding the human condition is that men live in secondhand worlds.

The consciousness of men does not determine their existence; nor does their existence determine their consciousness. Between the human consciousness and material existence stand communications and designs, patterns and values which influence decisively. . . .

C. Wright Mills
The Man in the Middle
Design and Human Problems, 1958

Peter Collinson, the Quaker merchant and naturalist in London writes testily to John Bartram in the colonies: "If thee know anything of thy own knowledge please to communicate it. The hearsay of others can't be depended on."

Loren Eiseley
The Firmament of Time, 1960

The Neotechnic order, if it means anything at all, with its better use of resources and population towards the bettering of man and his environment together, means these as a business proposition—the creation, city by city, region by region, of its Eutopia, each a place of effective health and well-being, even of glorious, and in its way unprecedented, beauty, this beginning here, there and everywhere—even where our Paleotechnic disorder seems to have done its very worst.

Patrick Geddes
Paleotechnic and Neotechnic
Cities in Evolution, 1913

"The difference between our decadence and the Russians' is that while theirs is brutal, ours is apathetic. We have an oral culture, a verbal culture, a culture of babel, bedlam and bickering. It's probably the final decline. . . ."

James Thurber
Manchester Guardian, February 1961

A Town is a tool.

Towns no longer fulfil this function. They are ineffectual; they use up our bodies, they thwart our souls.

The lack of order to be found everywhere in them offends us; their degradation wounds our self-esteem and humiliates our sense of dignity. They are not worthy of the age; they are no longer worthy of us.

Le Corbusier
translated by Frederick Etchells
The City of Tomorrow and Its Planning, 1925

To a greater extent than perhaps any other nation, we Americans have become an "Indoor" people. A large portion of our lives—working, sleeping, playing—is spent in buildings: buildings over whose design and construction we have little or no control; buildings whose physical and economic distribution are only remotely conditioned by our needs; buildings whose effect upon our health and happiness is only obscurely understood. Yet the impact of American buildings upon every aspect and area of American life can scarcely be over-emphasized.

James Marston Fitch, Jr.
Preface, *American Building: The Forces That Shape It,* 1948

An equal challenge is the tremendous urban growth that lies ahead. Within fifteen years our population will rise to 235,000,000 and by the year 2000 to 300,000,000 people. Most of this increase will occur in and around suburban areas. We must begin now to lay the foundations for livable, efficient and attractive communities of the future.

Land adjoining urban centers has been engulfed by urban development at the astounding rate of about 1,000,-000 acres a year. But the result has been haphazard and inefficient suburban expansion, and continued setbacks in the central cities' desperate struggle against blight and decay. Their social and economic base has been eroded by the movement of middle and upper income families to the suburbs, by the attendant loss of retail sales, and by the preference of many industrial firms for outlying locations.

Our policy for housing and community development must be directed toward the accomplishment of three basic national objectives:

First, to renew our cities and assure sound growth of our rapidly expanding metropolitan areas.

Second, to provide decent housing for all of our people.

Third, to encourage a prosperous and efficient construction industry as an essential component of general economic prosperity and growth.

President Kennedy
Special message to Congress on housing and community development
March 10, 1961

1

EROSION OF THE HUMAN HABITAT

EROSION OF THE HUMAN HABITAT

Dilemma of Quantity

The human population of the world and its productive capacity are reaching dimensions that defy the individual imagination. Today billions of people are demanding accommodations of all kinds, moving at ever greater speeds, communicating over vast distances in no time at all, and urbanizing at astonishing densities. The sudden extension of quantities alone has produced disorientation, confusion, terror, and anarchy. Swept up in this fantastic dynamic of his own making, man is apt to see only segments of the horizon at a time and, inversely, compounds his difficulties by not looking deeply into the smaller maelstrom of beginnings where he might find clues for unity. Man has not yet developed a strategy for organizing huge quantities although he has perfected techniques for computing them.

The glitter and debilitating chaos of mass culture— Henry Miller's "air-conditioned nightmare"—is advancing at the same rate as human population and technical developments. And not only is the advance in population and technology bound to continue, but economists and scientists declare that it will do so with increasing acceleration. On the evidence, one may reasonably anticipate still greater chaos.

These are problems in no way new to the philosopher and scientist, but recently the uneasiness has been spreading in proportion to the nightmare itself, and explicit discontent is being voiced in many unexpected places. Artists, newspaper, radio and TV reporters, entertainers and businessmen, even housewives are voicing concern over the public good instead of exclusively promoting their private gains or comforts. Planning issues are becoming political issues as hot as private property. (Outraged by the present situation, even some designers, less docile than the run of the mill, have joined the angry chorus of discontent and dissent.)

In this book some problems in making the human habitat, and in shaping man's physical environment, are tackled head-on in the belief that if the special contemporary characteristics of the physical environment are recognized, at this eleventh hour, the task of designing can be advanced in a forthright way and further erosion of the human habitat can be prevented.

Organizing Principles

A new physical urban order is needed to give expression and meaning to the life of "urbanizing" man, to clarify, to define, to give integrity to human purposes and organization, and finally, to give these *form*.

Today modern cities and other man-made elements in the physical environment are becoming shapeless for lack of an informing principle. But no such principle will be forthcoming, and no action will be taken, until the processes of design are themselves informed and controlled by the recognition of new realities.

The State of Urbanism

While failing to produce satisfactory new environments we are losing the best of the old. Ancient, powerful symbols and images—unique and irreplaceable places, buildings, many memorials, and entire historic cities, man's most telling evidence of a communal way of life—are being neglected or totally destroyed. And modern man seems unable to produce their modern equivalents. In the historic city squares, modern wheeled traffic is crowding out the people and such monuments as the great civic fountains of the past. The statue of Eros, once the delight of strolling visitors to Piccadilly Circus, has become unreachable and can be properly seen only on a penny postcard. In almost every city the pleasure of participation in city life through leisurely pedestrian movement is lost in the turmoil of cars. There may indeed come a time when travel and communication, if left unchecked, will make the city environment so diffuse that active urban life as it was will disappear. It is even possible that unused leisure and purposeless mobility will be so abundant that they will kill all but museum experience of the city-born arts. The comprehension of events, and the delight in beauty, that humanity, rich and poor alike, may derive from its physical environment cannot be achieved in a condition of anarchy.

The visual arts in Western society as implements to be used toward these ends have once again become a focus of concern and are in process of being reinstated as man's highest achievement. But however informed civilized man may appear to be when faced with paintings and sculpture of modest dimensions, he becomes bewildered when confronted by the large dimensions of cityscape and landscape. Since the larger scale seems too much for him, and too complex for him to comprehend, he is apt to respond arbitrarily, or simply ignore the problem, or even deny that city and country spaces can be made into effective environments for the activity they contain.

Sudden Obsolescence

It is not, however, impossible to reverse this trend and to conceive a more constructive role for planning. Man is fully capable of coping with the large scale, of solving complex problems, of producing environments that could help reshape humanity for the better. But to do this he must first recognize the dominant circumstances of the present urban culture and how they affect him.

He must recognize that the diverse pieces of civilized man's habitat—cities, towns, constellations, clusters, streets, arteries, parks, squares, houses, apartments, dwellings, shelters, call them what you will—have become obsolete. We believe that any further attempt to design in the conventional way, without a careful fresh look at the problem, and the help of some defensible basic principle, will do little more than add another set of shapes to the growing catalogue of architectural millinery.

The New Invaders

A reshaped environment, a new sense of urbanity, will not rise of itself, for it is not the inevitable end or by-product of technological and economic abundance. Ever since Henry Ford sent the first mass-produced cheap transportation rolling in and out of towns, and in particular since the Second World War, the accelerated dissolution of the pre-industrial epoch has been spreading to the ends of the earth. Although the real advantages of mechanized transportation and electronic communications could bring genuine prosperity to underdeveloped countries, what has actually become visible and audible are the all too familiar symbols of American success: ubiquitous loudspeakers, cars, gadgets, and mechanical noise. Mankind's newly found mobility, the independence given by the private car, the insatiable ear for broadcasts, and the mania for numberless labor-saving devices, have all changed civilized lives more deeply than has so far been suspected.

At first the products of the new technology were treated as a series of conveniences which the larger fabric of the town or house could absorb without disturbance, but there are far deeper scars left on the environment than most of us care, or dare, to admit. Many of the features of the good life that are most conspicuously missing today are precisely those that have been swamped by technology. The mechanical comforts and marvels invited into civilized homes are interfering with human lives in the manner of "The Man Who Came to Dinner."

Above all, a precious ingredient of the past is in danger

of rapid extinction: privacy, that marvelous compound of withdrawal, self-reliance, solitude, quiet, contemplation, and concentration.

The Search for Privacy

It is the contention of this book that only through the restored opportunity for firsthand experience that privacy gives can health and sanity be brought back to the world of the mass culture.

Privacy is most urgently needed and most critical in the place where people live, be it house, apartment, or any other dwelling. The dwelling is the little environment into which all the stresses and strains of the large world are today intruding, in one way or another, ever more deeply. To serve the best interests of privacy two of these stresses in particular, traffic and noise, must be treated as invaders. We shall describe a special kind of urban dwelling in which these invaders, whether they come from the outside or from within, cannot interfere with privacy.

It is our further contention that to contain this kind of dwelling, and to develop both privacy *and* the true advantages of living in a community, an entirely new anatomy of urbanism is needed, built of many hierarchies of clearly articulated domains. Such an urban anatomy must provide special domains for all degrees of privacy and all degrees of community living, ranging from the most intimately private to the most intensely communal. To separate these domains, and yet allow their interaction, entirely new physical elements must be inserted between them. It is because these new elements of separation emerge as vital and independent units in their own right that a new urban order may develop from the hierarchy of domains.

Only when the habitat of urbanizing man is given such an order shall we perhaps restore to urban life a fruitful balance between community and privacy.

VANISHING NATURE

Sabotaging the Wilderness Bill

It was bad enough that the House Committee on Interior and Insular Affairs yesterday reported a substitute Wilderness Bill that perverts the purpose of the legislation . . . it is a slap in the face to all the fine conservation organizations and to countless individual citizens who have worked long and hard for the preservation of America's dwindling remnants of wild and scenic splendor.

. . . the Wilderness Bill is the most important piece of conservation legislation before the present Congress.

New York *Times*, August 31, 1962

By taking a certain amount of trouble you might still be able to get yourself eaten by a bear in New York State. . . . Solitude is receding at the rate of four and a half kilometers per annum.

Aldous Huxley

Tomorrow and Tomorrow and Tomorrow, 1956

The more I see of life the more I perceive that only through solitary communion with nature can one gain an idea of its richness and meaning. I know that in such contemplation lies my true personality, and yet I live in an age when on all sides I am told

exactly the way through which life can be developed. Am I an exception, a herd outcast? There are also solitary bees, and it is not claimed that they are biologically inferior.

Cyril Connolly

The Unquiet Grave, 1945

At the National Institutes of Health, in Bethesda, John C. Calhoun allowed litter-mates to grow up in one large pen, where every rat had an individual food hopper. From the start, when eating, they huddled like a farrow at a single hopper; later, though free to roam, eat, and nest in four intercommunicating pens, these rats and their descendants spent most of their time in one of the four, and as I write this they are still there paying for their sociability in lowered fertility and shortened lives. For his part, my friend Calhoun coined a phrase that deserves to outlive his rats, and is still musing on *pathological togetherness*.

Edward S. Deevey

The Hare and the Haruspex:

A Cautionary Tale

Yale Review, December 1959

Although we cheerfully speak about *the* environment of an organism or a population, we know well there is no such thing. A population of individuals lives in a range of environments, narrow or wide as the case may be; and adaptability is just as much a matter of being adapted to environments which differ from place to place as to environments which change from time to time.

Peter Brian Medawar

Reith Lectures, 1959

The Future of Man, 1960

Wilderness Invaded

Elderly persons who regret the passing of the urbane way of life have observed with equal pain the increasing penetration of the countryside by the car, the helicopter's invasion of the wilderness, and the disappearance of plants and beasts they loved well. They have witnessed the passing of many intimate contacts with nature which, like the arts, once gave them unequaled pleasure.

In the not too distant future, man will have invaded every corner of the earth. Then, when the wilderness has vanished, even temporary escape from the city will also vanish. Man is in double jeopardy: at the same time that he risks the loss of the few lingering sophisticated pleasures of the historic city, he also risks losing the comfort of occasional direct contacts with unspoiled nature; for under the heels of crowds and the constant movement of wheels, the natural beauty of the wilderness atrophies as quickly as the man-made beauty of the ancient city.

No environment, natural or man-made, can withstand the presence and sound of crowds and machines that it was not intended to accommodate. Even the best attempts at conservation are defeated by the intruding quantities of men and vehicles. The familiar shiny automobiles parked in the great game preserve of Kruger Park in South Africa are merely a more vivid version of the tragedy of tourist buses in the piazzas of Tuscany or Coca-Cola barges on the Grand Canal of Venice.

Dissolving Contrast

Escape to the wilderness, if it is to be a successful experience, demands a sense of total isolation from other human beings. But even the most grueling efforts of removal to the most remote and wild pockets of the world are increasingly rewarded with the sudden discovery of the other man's canoe, helicopter, camp site, or party, and the sound of his voice, gun, or outboard motor.

Opportunity for direct contact with nature is not only hard to find in its ideal wilderness form, it is becoming increasingly difficult for any but a wealthy minority to experience nature in the local countryside through a brief foray or "day in the country." After crossing the barrage of suburbia the city dweller encounters the barriers of private ownership, forcing him either to trespass or to join the other trippers and picnickers on limited and heavily trodden public land.

The "status" house in the country, with its generous protective acreage, has long been the solution of the few better shod, but adequate land is no longer available. A new equivalent, however—the promise of mobility—may become the prerogative of far greater numbers in the future, bringing ever vaster problems of conservation with it. New packages of energy, water regeneration, climate control, and radio communication will give dwellings a degree of autonomy that will allow them to be almost anywhere. Possibly when the techniques of autonomy are well established, the fixed autonomous *house* will give way, in its turn, to some form of autonomous *mobile shelter*. (The present popularity of the trailer suggests that its advantages are highly appealing.) Hordes of mobile homes will then follow the changing seasons (real or induced) and bring traffic jams and ash cans even to the desert and the jungle.

Expanding Control

This gloomy picture is already partly realized. The marks of man's penetration are everywhere. Contact with nature is hard to find not only because of man's expanding presence but because of his expanding control and transformation of nature itself. The courses of rivers are being changed, their waters contained in man-made lakes;

mountains are being moved and tunneled, land claimed from the sea; rain and snow and even whole climates are now subject to control. The purely natural is shrinking while the man-made is growing. No one can tell one from the other, and soon there may be no difference anywhere.

Given his vast potential for control, man has the opportunity to reverse the predominantly destructive pattern of the past. Yet, only "yesterday" civilized countries were losing forests and turning fertile country into deserts of dust and desolation. No sooner had they learned painfully to control plant ecology through forestry than they launched into a new interference program; today they are experimenting on a far wider variety of life forms through biochemical means. The cumulative effect of such interference with the environment does not change only ecological patterns; it destroys them. It even appears possible that man could manage, with his wastes, to pollute the supposedly infinite sea just at the moment when he is learning to utilize its vast resources.

A New Ecology

Within a few years human intervention will be sufficiently expanded to affect the whole human species; and man, if he is to survive, will face the inescapable need to design an all-embracing ecology of his own; even, perhaps, the need to transform himself. Accelerating population growth, interference with and mastery over the natural, will make man's escape from man wholly impossible, and will force him to accept responsibility for every phenomenon on the surface of the earth. He will have to design and build his own ecology, his own adaptation to the environment of his own making.

Until he recognizes the more subtle and devastating aspects of his complacent submission to "human nature," he cannot begin to prepare for this responsibility in terms of human engineering. First, he can and must be responsible for the physical form of the environment that is to be the framework for his ecology.

Either he must learn to preserve the existing equilibrium of life or he must introduce a new equilibrium of his own making. If he does neither, his present unplanned conduct may deform human nature beyond all cure, even if it manages to survive the more violent holocausts. The threat of sudden destruction is more dramatic but not more severe.

Man's responsibility in the face of global urbanization is to make every urban form part of a fully functioning environmental system which contains the full balance and equilibrium that such a system demands. Man was responsible in the past for the development of whole cities as coherent environments, but was only dimly aware of this fact through a preoccupation with buildings, streets, squares, statuary—the concrete aspects of the city. A balanced environment was provided by immediate contact with surrounding untouched nature. Today it is becoming clear that the whole environment, as form, poses problems of quite a new order of complexity.

Awakening appreciation of the need to design fully functioning self-contained environments, capable of sustaining human life over long periods, is perhaps best seen in the development of military and space programs.

The Capsule Syndrome

Both the nuclear submarine and the space capsule have been designed to support life over protracted periods without the possibility of escape. It is already clear that there are very special problems associated with the design of such total environments. The designers of space capsules have observed that the technical problems of providing food and air and other physical necessities are trivial beside the problem of keeping the capsule's inhabitants human. The greatest difficulty seems to be the stress of confinement. The totally man-made character of the capsule environment and the inability to escape appear to produce unbearable nervous stress.

At present humanity can still escape from man-made cities. But when man assumes responsibility for the whole earth, and the control of every part of it, a syndrome comparable to that found in the capsule may develop. An urban form that would properly reflect all the pressures of our time would be capable of sustaining balanced life within it, without need for escape. It would be a fully functioning framework for ecological equilibrium. Only thoughtful design can help deter further mayhem. If the design problem is solved there will be no capsule syndrome.

3

DISSOLVING CITY

The gamut of choice between extremes is curtailed if the city has an inappropriate form. Every lack of differentiation in its physical pattern means a negation of choice, and thus a negation of true urbanity. An inhuman anonymity then results, that of particles in an amorphous mass, whereas a genuinely urbane anonymity is comparable to the full splendor of the whole without losing any of its own lustre.

Edouard Sekler

Daedalus, Summer 1960

For this is the first taste of the blue mosques of Iran. I shall never be able to forget the moment of sighting that blue dome again, losing it, and seeing it once more near enough to catch the china gleam of light on it. And now, while one holds one's breath, the golden dome appears. A wide street or boulevard has been cleared in a circle round these two buildings, the Shrine of the Imam Reza and the Mosque of Gauhad Shad. The Shrine has a golden dome shaped like a helmet and a pair of minarets plated with gold; while the dome of the Mosque is blue—but what shade of blue is it? For it changes colour. It alters with the hour. One could, and does, walk round that boulevard for hours on end.

Sacheverell Sitwell

Arabesque and Honeycomb, 1957

OAKLAND: "When you get there, there is no there, there."

Gertrude Stein

Reported by a guide

DISSOLVING CITY

Some people are old enough to have enjoyed the life of urbanity that existed in the well-defined, individual cities of the past. They remember these cities as possessing forms and characteristics which were peculiar to each, as being capable of rousing memorable delights or even positive— not apathetic—dislike. Urbane men it is true made forays outside into the more natural world. The available contrast of the two worlds enriched the experience of each. But they could then return with renewed zest to the environment of their own making which was able to give them nourishment and pleasure.

Most people today find pleasure and satisfaction in an ancient city which possesses visible physical evidence of its individual origin, growth, and purpose. It is a unique and personal expression of the activity and life within. An urban environment of this kind is deeply felt; the inhabitants subconsciously respond to specific visual experiences with a sense of belonging, identification, and affection. Civic beauty, as a whole, is consciously shared and does much to induce feelings of loyalty, pride, and patriotism. So strong are these visible features of urbanity that even a stranger, a visitor, cannot escape their impact.

Such cities possess physical clarity because their forms emerged in direct response to relatively simple limited pressures. Cultural continuity and slow technological change combined to establish a planning and building method that relied on adjustment and refinement through trial and error. A pressure needed only to be felt to find its way into form; any aspect of the form that failed was bound to be weeded out in time. This interaction between the inhabitants, the social purpose, and the manner of building gave each city its identity.

Purpose, Order, Plan

An example of direct translation of pressure into form may be seen in defensive towns like Naarden: the encircling bastions are the direct expression of the need to fortify the town against the cross fire of the newly invented cannon.

The Roman camp form, as seen at Aosta, developed from the need for Roman troops to garrison captured territory. This form, a cross with each quadrant subdivided by another cross, made the internal administration and supervision of the town extremely simple and minimized the risk of revolt.

The form of Amsterdam is clearly a response to the pressures of trade, which required that seagoing barges circulate freely among the burghers' houses.

Pikillacta, the Inca store town, grew up as the node of a widely scattered agricultural society. It was Inca policy to provide security for the surrounding villagers. This form of town is given its articulation by the need for efficient storage, supervision, and distribution of supplies.

The nested form of Peking's northern half, the Tartar City surrounding the Imperial City which in turn surrounds the Forbidden City, is principally determined by the sanctity of the emperor and the pressures of custom and ritual demanding various degrees of association with his person.

Order and Delight

These cities were well-defined wholes; they were clearly organized internally, and each stood in clear relation to its natural environment. The particular order made each city readily identifiable. Less fortunate modern man can but envy their present-day inhabitants for the memorable focal points preserved, and the perfect placement of these cities within their respective landscapes; can share with them the satisfaction that comes from something known

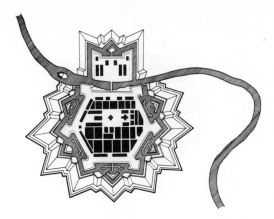

Fortified Town, Naarden

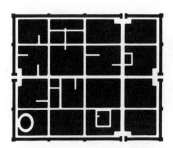

Roman Camp, Aosta

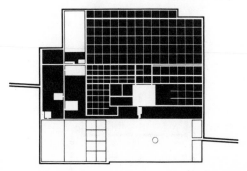

Inca Store Town, Pikillacta

Nördlingen

Amsterdam

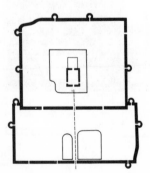

Peking

and understood. The fan-shaped piazza of Siena and its cathedral's eminence, the canals and bridges of Venice, or Amsterdam, call to mind pleasures of a special kind.

The above descriptions of the governing principle, or pressures, behind the city plans are, of course, convenient oversimplifications. Often even these rather simple organizations were the response to several kinds of pressure acting simultaneously. For example, Siena reflects its religious life, civic organization, and system of trade as well as the need for defense. Nevertheless the direct relation between form and pressure, and the slow process of development, generated a clear plan.

Conflicting Pressures

Today the effect of pressures on form has become peripheral and indirect instead of central and direct as it was in those earlier days. The net of pressures on the modern industrial city is so vast, and includes so many conflicts of priority, that during the course of their action on form the relationships between pressure and form become distorted, and the resultant forms are at variance with the original pattern of pressures. For example, the automobile which was developed as a tool to serve human purposes has emerged as a dominant pressure in its own right. The forms which result, such as the strips of roadway commerce that are the main streets of many modern cities, are in conflict with their original basic human purposes. The architectural space of a predominantly pedestrian civilization—shaded alleyways and quiet squares standing in contrast to festive and busy streets, or to solemn and monumental avenues and plazas—has become secondary to the automobile, its accommodating tarmac and flanking commerce. The automobile needs accommodation. But so do people's other needs. At present the form of the city reflects only one, and excludes the other.

Feeble Focus

The city core is becoming decentralized as a civic center from the point of view of administrative convenience and availability of services such as schools, hospitals, and fire stations. It is becoming equally decentralized for the purposes of commerce dealing in staples. City stores are giving way to shopping centers which cater to their increasing number of consumers, with greater economy to themselves and greater convenience to the public, in more readily accessible locations "plugged into" rapid transportation systems outside the city proper.

The result is that the urban environment, growing under the accumulation of diffuse and contradictory needs, each year becomes less clearly organized; there are fewer and fewer and weaker and weaker focal points, or visual events, which can help the inhabitant orient himself. The only clear visual organization of the subway is the subway map. The actual connections of the subway to the city have no clarity whatsoever, and bear no visible relation to the environment: as you emerge from the subway exit you don't know which way to turn. Every street intersection of the lifeless grid plan and every basement connection to a building is the same as every other. Every throughway exit, every cloverleaf is standardized. Written directions are our only guides, and they are not sufficient for immediate orientation.

The Crude Outline

The contemporary urban picture not only lacks clarity; it is crude, composed of coarse outline and color. The monotony of loudness prevails. Subtleties of line, tone, and texture, which reveal the artist's hand, are all but invisible. The urban melting pot promises little more significance than mere gigantism, aggressive upward thrusting skyscrapers and flashing neon lights. The skyscraper, born of land scarcity and the invention of the elevator, is all too often constructed where land is not yet in critical supply or when function is not improved by vertical organization. Neon lights are fast losing their significance in a profusion of signs of identical visual aspect and force, and, together with traffic lights, vanish from sight. Man has produced a paradox of "protective coloring." The things he wants to be seen most clearly are becoming invisible because there are so many of them. The mass-produced are dominant. Particular and unique flavors have been dissolved in the muddy solution of the modern city and can no longer be tasted or enjoyed.

Urban Litter

Just as the internal organization of our formless and sprawling cities has been destroyed, our cityscapes have lost any proper relation to the surrounding landscape and the larger environment of which they are an organic part. The seashore, the rivers, the valleys, which once nurtured and gave our cities being, or the hills, which protected them from enemies and floods, mean yearly less and less. The city's edges are being frayed and made unclear. The bits and pieces of urban wear and tear are drifting farther and farther out until what was once known as countryside is now a repository for urban litter. Calling the city, its periphery and suburbs together, a metropolitan region does not endow them with a visible satisfying order.

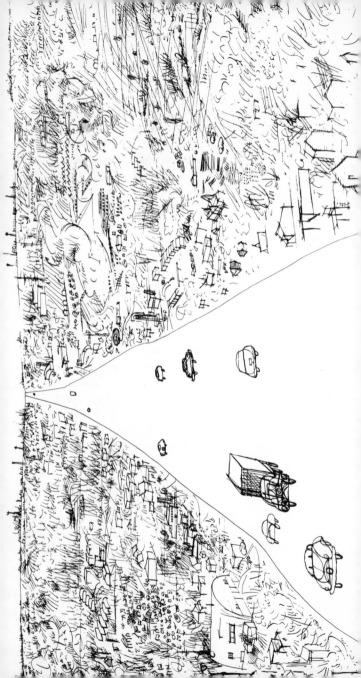

4

THE SUBURBAN FLOP

The art of building cannot be more grand than it is useful; nor its dignity a greater praise than its convenience.

Isaac Ware
A Complete Study of Architecture
1756

When I was a boy, my family was living in a city apartment with open gas-jets, individual coal-heated stoves in each room, including the bathroom, where warm water was heated for the bath each Saturday: that took two hours.

There was no electric streetcar, no automobile, of course, no plane.

Radio, film, gramophone, X-ray, telephone were nonexistent.

Walter Gropius
Design and Industry, 1950

The Binneys were among the first New York City dwellers to move to Old Greenwich, a decision that prompted members of their family to think "we were a pair of lunatics," Mrs. Binney said.

Mrs. Edwin Binney Dies:
Led Suburbia Migration
New York *Herald Tribune,* 1960

I'm moving back to New York, and I can't wait. Those fierce canyons hold no terrors for me: I've known the battlefield of Suburbia, and I'm not going to reenlist.

Mary McLaughlin
Good-by Suburbs, *Today's Living*
New York *Herald Tribune,* 1958

THE SUBURBAN FLOP

Best of Both Worlds

Nature is vanishing. The city is vanishing. The accelerating dissolution of both ideal nature and ideal city has induced a massive compromise, an attempt to salvage elements of both. In the early stages of the industrial revolution the urban magnet attracted country people into towns with the promise of jobs, variety and excitement, creating an inward flow. The reverse outward flow of disillusioned city dwellers escaping from congestion, degradation, and squalor, and in search of a privately owned "house in the country," has been going on ever since transportation made it possible. At first the privilege of the few, it has now become the compulsion of the many. The suburb, camp follower of technocratic culture, is spreading from the United States to the most distant corners of the earth with its myth of providing in a single package the convenience of the town house and the enjoyments of the country house. But both the pseudo city and the pseudo country, with commuters shuttling between them in a desperate search for satisfaction which neither can provide, appear in the end to promote little more than discontent. The suburb's promise of country life within easy reach of the pleasures of the city has proved false.

Nevertheless, for the present, the suburban environment seems likely to survive and expand; the wish to have one's cake and eat it is still strong. The desire to opt for the best of both possible worlds propounded by Ebenezer Howard, author of *Garden Cities of Tomorrow*, in the late nineteenth century still seems to find favor in the middle twentieth; but the perversion of his excellent principles continues.

Failure as Nature

Howard's original amalgam of "Town-Country" was intended to provide urban man with a set of very excellent conditions, a constant relationship with the natural world. Few would contest the basic goal. In a physical environment "fit for man to live in," in the fullest sense, humanity must be able to see, touch, smell, and hear other forms of life. The real pleasure of the earth, the weather, the scent of plants, and the songs of birds and insects, cannot be enjoyed except through unhurried contact. Human lives, and especially the life processes of families, are stimulated by the visible order of nature. To appreciate these other kinds of life, and to enjoy them fully, it is essential that the contact with them be continual. Occasional escapes into the wilderness, stimulating though they may be, are not the same. The little tree growing outside one's own room is a more real tree than the largest Sequoia in the national park. One becomes conscious of one's own development only against the pulse of the changing seasons and the recurrent rhythms of light and dark. All this demands dwellings close to the ground with easy access to outdoors, an organic whole in which indoors and outdoors are integrated in a single comprehensive shelter.

Pseudo Country

The suburban house not only fails in the many details of organization that we will discuss more fully later, but even fails to provide this outdoor life successfully. The pseudo country house sits uneasily in its shrunken countryside, neither quite cheek by jowl with its neighbor nor decently remote, its flanks unprotected from prying eyes and penetrating sounds. It is a ridiculous anachronism.

The view from the picture window is of the other man's picture window. The individually owned and independently maintained outdoor spaces lap around the house and dribble miserably over curb edges into the gutters of the street. The bare unused islands of grass serve only the myth of independence. This unordered space is neither town nor country; behind its romantic façade, suburbia contains neither the natural order of a great estate nor the man-made order of the historic city. What nature there is, neatly trimmed, standardized, bush by bush, flower by flower, is never free from its noisy, unnatural mechanical confinement. The richness of the best lawn or of the most prolific flowering hybrids pales before the splendor of the chrome-dazzling car. The finest young tree (young by necessity because the bulldozer takes precedence) is dwarfed by the full grown telegraph poles and the lianas of power lines.

Failure as City

The suburb fails to be a countryside because it is too dense. It fails to be a city because it is not dense enough, or organized enough. Countless scattered houses dropped like stones on neat rows of development lots do not create an order, or generate community. Neighbor remains stranger and the real friends are most often quite far away, as are schools, shopping and other facilities. The husband suffers the necessity of long-distance commuting, but the housewife who remains behind suffers the far greater pain of boredom. The housewife, or mother, for whom the suburb was intended, has become its greatest victim. Isolation in the vast sprawl of suburbia has led to a spiraling dependence on transportation and communication to provide contacts and experiences missing at home. The "little woman" finds herself either behind the wheel of a car, an unpaid chauffeur, or in front of the television set, a captive spectator.

Civilized man lives in a strange topsy-turvy world. People and places previously remote are now becoming part and parcel of an extended community whose effects on the dwelling were not foreseen when the suburban process began. Modern communications systems bring, however fragmented and fleetingly, glimpses of phenomena and sounds never before seen or heard. Man is in touch with the whole world without moving from his seat. But the man next door with different tastes, often expressed in diverse and loud noises, is all at once transformed from desirable neighbor into intrusive stranger. The suburb pays no attention to these closely linked overwhelming changes, and pretends to be a village of closely knit neighbors and friends. The men, women, and children of suburbia are seldom quite together, and never quite alone.

Complex and Invisible

The suburb aggravates its failure by refusing to relate to its technology. In a technically advanced society, neither town nor dwelling is any longer a self-contained unit. Its most vital and indispensable components are those that connect it to the larger environment and are hardly visible. Radio waves are totally invisible. Water, sewage, and power lines are for the most part hidden. Roadways, telephone poles, and spilling garbage cans, though ever present, are not seen by us because we have learned to overlook them.

The industrial society spends more and more of its house-dollar not on the visible spatial structure, on the buildings that are "Architecture" in its traditional sense, but on items of connection, circulation, communication, comfort, hygiene, all involving mechanical and electrical equipment. The dwelling has become essentially a cell in a complex organism—and must be seen as such if it is to correspond to either old or new realities. If man's habitat is not to become a malignant cancer it must be given a form reflecting its new function.

Travesty of Progress

It is because the industrial, commercial, and professional purveyors of housing shun responsibility for the larger organism and continue to provide nothing more than pseudo autonomous creations that our lives are so far out of joint. *A form that ignores its technical context cannot possibly accommodate the good life successfully.* Indeed, it is precisely because the significant advances of technology have been ignored that the good life is slipping through our fingers. Sophisticated, "up-to-date" techniques or new materials do not automatically improve performance. Synthetics and machinery obviously have their special qualities and proper place. But our ability to manufacture a plastic container the size of a house and then fill it with mechanical gadgets hardly commends itself as progress in housing if the plan serves obsolete purposes.

Dissolving Suburbs

Growing disillusionment with suburbia, with its debilitating sameness, with the wastefulness of commuting for those who are forced to spend at least a part of their life in cities, has led quite recently to the beginnings of a return to the city. In spite of growing decentralization, and the fact that more and more people with more and more cars live in the never-never land of Suburbia, most of the money continues to be earned and spent in the city proper. The affluent society is under constant pressure to buy something new, and the suburban shopping-center parking lot (and movie theater) is too limited in its range of choice to satisfy expanding appetites. In many cities retail centers (and recreation centers) through ambitious urban renewal programs are beginning to exploit their advantage. But while helping to revitalize the city, these centers still aggravate the overload of shuttling traffic. For a long time to come, one car out of the two in every ideal garage will, no doubt, continue to be a little private pig going to the central public market.

People want to be everywhere. The reason they moved out was to find the country and escape the disadvantages of the city. The reason they are moving back is that the country is no longer there and they would like to regain the advantages of the city. But when everything is everywhere, wherever you go there is nothing tangible to find.

Urban No Man's Land

Searching for a better amalgam of the man-made and the natural than suburbia provides, urban designers have now begun to replace the suburban no man's land with an urban no man's land. They have created low and high rise apartment blocks, free standing in their own "green" space, to create, through contrast, the illusion of country. Though the logic of this device seemed admirable at first, the enjoyment of such scattered green spaces has turned out to be largely illusory. They are not large enough to act as public parks, and not small enough to possess the intimate pleasure of the private garden. Everything belongs to everybody with the result that nothing actually belongs to, or is enjoyed by, anybody. Their ownership, administration, and maintenance is neither specifically public nor private. They are the left-over voids between gigantic boxes, where sparsely sprinkled adults and children are equally ill at ease. More often than not, even the plans that profess to have found the ideal solution squander available land by allocating it to questionable purposes, or more often still, to no real purposes at all.

The time may soon come when planners, designers, developers, and others will recognize and act on the simple notion that the spaces between buildings are as important to the life of urban man as the buildings themselves.

If the total land area were to be carefully planned for maximum use at every scale, the inner city could accommodate both vertical buildings for all-purpose use and short-term occupancy, *and* dwellings on the ground for families with children. Such dwellings on the ground could, as functioning parts of the urban technological context, succeed where suburbia has failed.

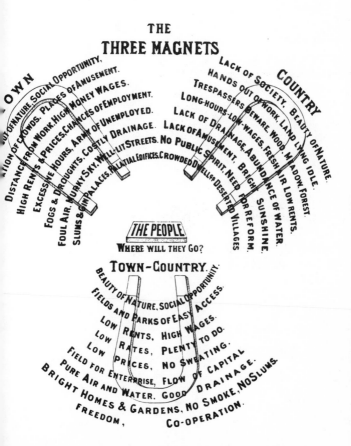

Diagram by Ebenezer Howard

5

IN SEARCH OF THE SMALL

Variety is not the spice of life; it is the very stuff of it.

Christopher Burney
Solitary Confinement, 1952

Modern man's feeling of isolation and powerlessness is increased still further by the character which all his human relationships have assumed. The concrete relationship of one individual to another has lost its direct and human character and has assumed a spirit of manipulation and in-strumentality.

Erich Fromm
Escape from Freedom, 1941

The suicide rate (23.4 per 100,000 inhabitants) is the highest in the world, and in the great majority of cases is attributed simply to *ense* (tired-ness with life).

Fosco Maraini
Meeting with Japan, 1959

. . . the sense of universal futility, the feelings of bore-dom and despair, with the complementary desire to be "anywhere, anywhere out of the world," or at least out of the place in which one hap-pens at the moment to be, have been the inspiration of poetry and the novel for a century and more. It would have been inconceivable in Matthew Green's day to have written a serious poem about ennui.

Aldous Huxley
Accidie, *On the Margin,* 1923

Indeed, the higher orga-nisms actively avoid a com-pletely monotonous environ-ment. A rat in a maze will use different routes to food, if they are available, rather than the same one all the time. It will tend to avoid areas in which it has spent considerable time and to explore the less familiar areas.

Woodburn Heron
Pathology of Boredom
Scientific American, January 1957

While economists are debat-ing whether any satiation level for income is possible, there is strong reason for belief that a saturation level for cultural interaction exists. A recent crop of psychological studies, which still need confirmation and extension, suggest that human physiological limits may be placed somewhere in the neighborhood of one bil-lion hubits per capita per year. As this limit is ap-proached people show signs of stress—apparent harassment, increased errors in actions, confusion, an expressed desire for escape, etc. An increasing

fraction of the urban population may be expected to
become subject to commu-
nications stress as the pace
quickens.

Richard L. Meier
Measuring Social and Cultural
Change in Urban Regions
*Journal of the American Institute of
Planners,* November 1959

A privacy, an obscure nook
for me. I want to be forgotten
even by God.

Robert Browning
Paracelsus, Part V, 1835

IN SEARCH OF THE SMALL

Lost Equilibrium

The effects of our present man-made environment, from which mankind may eventually not be able to escape, are brought home to us by the time-honored advice of the old-fashioned family doctor: "Take a holiday; what you need is a change." Latter-day medical practitioners in search of deeply hidden causes of discontent have added little to this diagnosis of modern urban man's chronic disease: the fundamental monotony of his anxiety-ridden existence.

Although civilization is constantly adding to excitement—real, simulated, and induced—a large part of the spectrum of experience is conspicuous by its absence. Less and less do the mechanized, mass-produced, and mass-consumed, the routinized and vicarious provide opportunities for firsthand experiences of different pitch, intensity, and scale. A genuine variety in daily experience is missing.

Extended and Deprived

Continuous, personal identity with people, things, and nature readily encountered in the daily round in the city and country of the pre-industrial era are rare. A synthetic world presents people, things, and events, which are either too impersonal or overdramatized. Economic growth appears to celebrate quantity and exalt it above quality. We must try to draw attention to the overlooked, though vital, commonplaces.

Everywhere wheels are turning at cross purposes to legs and other people's voices cut across our thoughts. The fast and the high-pitched have all but obliterated the slow and relaxed. The large and loud have overwhelmed the small and quiet. Extinct are the intimate, the special, the strange experiences of the great cities of the past where once the solitary, the adventurer, or the poet in camouflage could mingle at will with the crowd and find pleasure by very reason of his anonymity.

What was once a commonplace—the possibility of escape from the crowd for privacy and rest—has all but vanished. The crowds, once restricted to the streets and borders of the public domain, now follow unbidden into the solitary, private domain by means of electronic media intruding acoustically through the thin partition that fails to separate man from his noisy neighbor.

The Intruders

The earlier, coherently organized city was fortified against the invader and the relative anarchy of the larger countryside; the individual buildings and houses were heavily armed against rebels, robbers, and the stranger. These precautions, which were clearly expressed in plan and structure, have slowly given way under the influence of economic improvement and social discipline, implemented by the organized enforcement of law. The great sheets of easily shattered glass, the picture window, the absence of walls and fences are all symbols of a short-lived confidence in the efficacy of such things.

However *le cercle est bouclé*—civilization has come full circle. Now that law enforcers are largely engaged in wrestling with traffic problems, efficiency in protection appears to be diminishing, with the result that opportunities for invaders of the private realm are multiplying. And the robbers and strangers of the past have been joined by hoodlums and psychopaths, confidence men and salesmen, all seemingly equally respectable, turning up in standard clothes and standard cars.

As though protection against the actuality of direct assault were not problem enough, modern man has the infinitely more difficult problem of dealing with the other and more numerous intruders whose loudspeaker voices and multifarious noises ring in his ears and whose blurred images on the screen dance before his eyes.

The diversity of invaders able to beat a path to his door and into his presence, augmented by those who now can penetrate beyond, into his subconscious mind, has put an enormous strain upon modern man's capacity to maintain even a semblance of security at any level.

Anatomy of Privacy

The individual requires barriers against the sounds and sight of innumerable visitors, including the disembodied visitors of TV and radio selected by one or another member of the family. The family, in turn, must protect itself against the choices of its ever-increasing number of immediate neighbors; and the larger group must take a stand against the chaotic profusion outside its domain.

Only physical insulation against the dangers and pain of invasion—interruption by people, traffic, and noise— can inhibit chaos and confusion. Even within the theoretically protected family realm, the same pressures operate, on a modified scale, in such matters as modesty or conflict of activity and interest between persons of different ages and education. Where is the provision for relaxation, concentration, contemplation, introspection, healthy sensuousness, all of which are conducive to intimacy, tenderness, wonder, and delight? If the individual cannot at least sometimes shut out the crowd-noise, how shall he notice and become fully reassured by the sounds of a child at play or the sight and sound of a bird as it signals the season's change?

Which Scale Is Human

Man talks of "humanity" glibly, if a little nervously, and is so accustomed to hearing the cliché, the human scale, that he does not pause to ask which human, at what time, where, under what conditions, is being measured. Yet this abstracted "human" now ranges through his technological extensions from the historic pedestrian-equestrian man, who built the most memorable monuments to his own scale, to the motorized or jet-propelled, "greater than speed of sound" giant who strides across his habitat in thousand league boots, his eyes on ever-widening horizons, but alas, in the process, trampling much underfoot.

R. Buckminster Fuller has commented that a visitor from Mars, descending to earth, would not see its inhabitants at all until he was almost on the earth's surface. Long before he saw them he would see highways, railroads, electric pylons, airports, buildings, and all the moving vehicles around them. He would perhaps be confused by this and mistake the great number of moving objects for this planet's inhabitants. Human inhabitants are in a similar position. Man sees man at his own scale more and more rarely. He sees him in the city and on the highways, and on the two dimensional techniscreen. He hears him on the telephone and over loudspeakers. But it is not until he so to to speak "uncorks" himself from these various contrivances that he is exposed as a real living being. It is only then, when he is in his unique natural condition, "face to face" with another that the historic scale relationship between his own physical structure, that of his fellows, and the dimension of his immediate environment is to be found, and only then that genuine intercourse becomes possible.

Large, Fast, and Loud

Mechanized, industrialized man has enormously amplified his senses by his inventions. With the help of instruments his vision penetrates vast distances and he can perceive both enormous and minute dimensions. Speeds and distances are brought within his reach that even the aeronauticists of thirty years ago did not dream of. But fascination for the new has all but eradicated interest in the old and the familiar. Focused on the exciting and the extreme, man is becoming indifferent to average dimensions, although these are the dimensions of humankind. The charm of the small has been transformed into the cult of the cute; indifference has become contempt. Moreover, for the man in the street, not involved in chemistry or nuclear physics, the minute has but partial interest. Only the "supercolossal," such as a manned vehicle sent to the moon, or the shocking, such as a ghastly murder committed round the corner, really hold him.

Loud noises and fast movement, now easily obtained and easily used, crowd out the soft and slow. The volume of the radio can always be turned up to shut out other sounds; the gas pedal can always be pushed down to intimidate slower, weaker travelers. In the process of building his mechanical extensions, man has all but lost himself. His medium stature and limited physical capacity are dwarfed by those of his own structures and machines; his natural voice is hardly ever heard above the din of machinery and the mechanical enlargements of natural sounds.

Unseen Damage

Science has provided means for measuring the damage done to man by unsuitable climate, dirt, or deprivation of basic physical necessities. But science is not as yet equipped, apparently, to measure the damage done by the nervous strain resulting from chronic exaggeration, or to assess man's adaptation, or lack of it, to similar violent and sudden changes in his condition caused by new technology. Life on an air-conditioned mountain top —for instance, the most luxurious skyscraper penthouse, where man is limited to large, dramatic, distant views, where he hears only loudspeaker sounds, where he cannot risk exposure to the weather—is severely monochromatic. Overstimulation at the high, loud, fast end of the spectrum of experience, and deprivation at the low, quiet, slow end is robbing man of balanced variety. Attention is focused largely on the conspicuous dramatic inessentials: the new records, the fastest race, the highest building, the brightest lights, "the first time," the farthest shot, the loudest noise, the biggest audience, the prettiest girl, the largest fortune.

The apparent increase in variety in our wealthy, industrialized society may turn out to be a new form of monotony of mass-produced commodities. More and more becomes less and less, and mere quantity and repetition of individually stimulating events kills their effectiveness. The kaleidoscope of brilliant colors spins into the monochrome gray of the color wheel.

Pathology of Boredom

If man is restricted to one extreme, subjected exclusively to the excitement of the large scale, without the contrast of relief of the minuscule, it is easily conceivable that the human organism might atrophy. Human sensibility, which may be seriously blunted by monotonous overstimulation, may also be blunted if it is exercised exclusively in an environment of calculated and automatically controlled physical comfort. Our faculties function best and are best maintained at peak sharpness when effort is required of them.

Monotony of any kind—dull or intense—is debilitating. Boredom is a word heard commonly today. It may be that the uniformity of the "air-conditioned nightmare" fatigues both mind and body, that under such conditions the vital side of human life degenerates.

Possibly science will find that this balanced variety is not essential to man's physical well-being, but it seems unlikely. Equilibrium provided in nature for living organisms appears to be a compound of contrasts in a dynamic relationship. The man-made world must provide at least the same. Today it is prevented from doing so because of two conspicuous invaders. The very instruments that have given man increased dynamic power—total mobility and instantaneous communication—are destroying the equilibrium in the human habitat.

ENEMY NUMBER ONE: CAR

Mobile Man

Man on Wheels

Autocentric Culture

Town or Tarmac

Costly Cars

Obsolete Feet

Where Will Johnny Walk?

The Deadly Street

So politically dominant is the automobile that cities and states will tax and tear themselves apart in the effort to "do something" about traffic, but only through measures that facilitate (in effect, increase) the flow of vehicles, never reduce it. The result of each new palliative parkway is only to relieve some roads at the expense of others, inducing more people to drive more cars in an endless vicious circle.

To date, the car has revolutionized patterns of land use faster than theoretical conceptions of social time and distance have evolved to keep up with it, with the result that it bears many of the marks of an institution out of control, intractable to previous disciplines and impervious to moralizing.

David Riesman and Eric Larrabee
Autos in America, *Consumer Behavior—Research on Consumer Reactions*, 1958

HELL ON WHEELS: Special tonight: 7:30–8:30, Channel 2. Commuters–Strap hangers – Sunday Drivers – all agree it's a mess. Just step out the front door and you're right in the middle of it—a strangling paralysis of road and rail that each year brings the nation's fastest moving city closer to a dead stop. Have we come to the end of the line or is there a cure? Stay home tonight–see WCBS–TV's penetrating survey of the New York transportation crisis which affects every single person in the metropolitan area and ultimately the nation.

CBS Advertisement
New York *Herald Tribune*
July 18, 1960

A twenty-one-year-old girl wheeling a baby carriage in Brooklyn yesterday, pushed her baby to safety before she was crushed to death beneath the wheels of an automobile which mounted the sidewalk.

New York *Herald Tribune*
September 10, 1960

Lafayette, La., June 1, 1960 —The Most Rev. Maurice Schexnayder, Roman Catholic Bishop of Lafayette, today issued an edict refusing Christian burial to Roman Catholics declared criminally negligent in fatal automobile accidents.

New York *Herald Tribune*
June 2, 1960

Nothing is more dramatically apparent than the inadequacy of transportation in our larger urban areas. The solution cannot be found only in the construction of additional urban highways—vital as that job is. Other means for mass transportation which use less space and equipment must be improved and expanded.

Accordingly, I have asked the administrator of the Housing and Home Finance Agency and the Secretary of Commerce to undertake an immediate and extensive study of urban transportation problems and the proper role of the Federal government in their solution.

President Kennedy
Special message to Congress on housing and community development, March 10, 1961

ENEMY NUMBER ONE: CAR

Mobile Man

Modern civilization moves enormous quantities of people, raw materials, and finished goods from place to place. Since it depends on this pumping action for its life, there is no prospect of abatement. A growing number of citizens of the United States spend a growing proportion of their time in movement, most of it in cars. Though it is not our purpose to discuss all aspects of this growing mobility we can read the writing in the sky and realize that the promise of new paths through the stratosphere, over and above the vapor trails of our own time, makes mobility so much an everyday affair that its faults are more difficult to see than ever.

Man on Wheels

Taste for wheeled motion is drummed into Americans almost from the moment they are born. After young parents have tasted the delights of the first toddling state, a remnant recognition of a stage in the development of *anthropus erectus,* they take a progressively dimmer view of walking or any slow movement whatever. The small child is quickly taught the use of wheels: the tricycle, scooter, bicycle follow each other in rapid succession, to be replaced in early adolescence by motorized scooters and finally the King Car itself. Even motorized grass mowers are beginning to move at hazardous speeds over the standardized lawn and may eventually require a new breed of highly trained jockey to ride them.

Autocentric Culture

It has long been the contention in America that it is every individual's privilege to bring his automobile into his living room, and to sacrifice all the advantages of other forms of transportation by allowing this single convenience to override every other consideration. Today's compulsive preoccupation with the car has made our culture so "auto-centric" that even its most obviously uncomfortable facts escape notice.

Town or Tarmac

With the exception of the great metropolis where life continues unabated around the clock, such as London, Paris, or New York City, one third or more of civilization's typical "urban-suburban" acreage is a tarmac desert that is hot, flooded, or icy, according to season. Relatively *idle between the short peak hours of traffic rush,* it constitutes an immensely costly overhead and an immense waste of the most precious land. Perhaps we should console ourselves with the thought of the great stoicism developed by the suburbanite as he sits, day after day in every city of the union in the peak-hour traffic jams—the daily routine of the car commuter. But the evidence is to the contrary: no virtues are bred behind the wheel, but rather new vices. The Enemy is any other driver and this hatred among equals has transformed the brotherhood of early motoring days. On the modern highway the good Samaritan is hard to find.

Costly Cars

If our present mood of more and more and more cars continues, the cost of housing them will outstrip our hitherto astonishing capacity to pay for this intensely promoted private appetite out of the public purse. The public space that both government and business have to provide "at the other end" for the storage and maneuver space of the private car—out on its probably minute mission—is considerable. The sum total of parking and road surfaces promises to grow immensely in the public and even the private realm; as land becomes more scarce and more expensive, the cost of parking space may eventually become prohibitive at both ends. Any vehicle when not moving is ineffectual. The larger proportion of a car's life is spent in immobility. The stationary car is not only inefficient and uneconomic, it is indecent. Any transportation system for city populations will be effective only if every vehicle is constantly moving. An average car requires some four hundred square feet of paved space, the equivalent of 25 per cent of the floor area now provided for the average American family's house. But the prices themselves, do not tell us the true cost of the car. Its true cost is that it causes the sacrifice of other means of transportation.

An interesting experiment is now under way in Sweden, the second most affluent society in the world. While reaching for 100 per cent motorization for its inhabitants, a car for every family, Sweden is simultaneously developing its urban transportation systems toward maximum efficiency. An ingredient, likely to become universally desirable, is included in this overall transportation strategy; the exclusion, by all means available to a democratic society, of the private automobile from the central city areas.

In pursuit of this admirable public objective at least one municipality will provide free public transportation for its citizens inside the city limits. A bus every ten minutes will be available everywhere within five minutes' walking. In the long run, it is evidently cheaper, in urban areas, to provide continuous free rides than to accommodate the sporadic stops and starts of the automobile.

There is nothing wrong with the car per se. What is wrong is the exaggerated use we make of it. Essentially a private convenience, it violates public interest in too many places. The immense investment of public money in roads, bridges, garages and parking prevents the development of all the other forms of transportation that would be more appropriate to different purposes and scales. It even prevents walking.

Obsolete Feet

If man had set out to eliminate walking altogether he could not have invented more ingenious ways of doing it. Indeed, walking is very nearly eliminated already. It is common habit nowadays to cover trivial distances in enormous cars—in spite of the maneuver difficulties and the perpetual search for parking space. Lewis Mumford has wryly commented on the fact that a 250 horsepower car takes as long to reach downtown today as a single horse and buggy did eighty years ago. Even so, car owners always drive rather than walk. Even amateur golfers drive from hole to hole in electric buggies instead of walking.

This devotion to the automobile has other bizarre and dangerous consequences. Slender police resources are stretched to the limits of effectiveness and temper by huge numbers of cars. The result? The war between the law and traffic now claims more time and effort than the war between the law and crime; the criminal, by putting himself at the wheel of a car, is able to do double battle.

Another curiosity happens by chance to concern privacy. Since it is so hard to find inside the houses of today, young couples seek it in their cars. The car, heated and air-conditioned, is not only a bus but a bedroom, offering far more opportunities for intimacy than the old-fashioned porch or the sofa by the TV screen.

Devotion to speed is evident in the scale and precision of the cloverleaf intersection designed with exquisite care and constructed at great expense by skilled highway engineers. Civilized man is so fascinated by the possibilities and consequences of high speed that he has all but lost his sense of discrimination and is careless of occurrences at slower speeds. The cloverleaf's regard for clarity and safety differs sharply from suburban crossings and blind corners where the same car moves perhaps more slowly but with no less danger to human life.

Where Will Johnny Walk?

Speeds are steadily increasing and nobody likes to go slowly anywhere. Car users in their rare pedestrian state stand back respectfully from the platform's edge to let the subway train go by, and watch the passing bus almost as carefully when they step off the sidewalk, yet they very rarely pay attention to the danger of the delivery truck or their neighbor's car maneuvering just outside the house and when they are behind the wheel themselves they all behave with equal callousness.

When the car is traveling on a go-go highway, its dangers are to some extent controllable—over-all traffic organization, speed limits, and police supervision are partially effective. But as this same car turns off the highway to the byways, and finally rolls to a standstill in the residential street where we live, control paradoxically diminishes. You may manage to escape the pack of wolves in the open but not in the sheep pen. Greater control is needed at slow speed, but there is in fact less; freight has not yet been sorted out from passengers, or vehicles from pedestrians. The spectacular speed crashes on the highways in which civilized men kill themselves by the carload fill the headlines and are horribly and vividly portrayed in illustrated weeklies, but little is made of the poignant death of a child playing by the cars parked in the street where the unprotected, innocent, untrained, and careless are to be found.

The Deadly Street

The street on which the houses grow is deadly. The public sidewalk made good sense before it was cut to pieces every few years to make way for the private driveway. Now it is a shambles of curbs and changing levels—an obstacle race for mothers with their baby buggies. The street itself is no longer a promenade for friends and neighbors among whom pleasant exchanges can take place, but a service artery carrying dangerous trucks and other high-smelling vehicles filled with strangers. It is no longer a place for a community of children at play, or strolling lovers. Nor is it fit for a dog. The unresolved conflict between pedestrians and vehicles has made it obsolete.

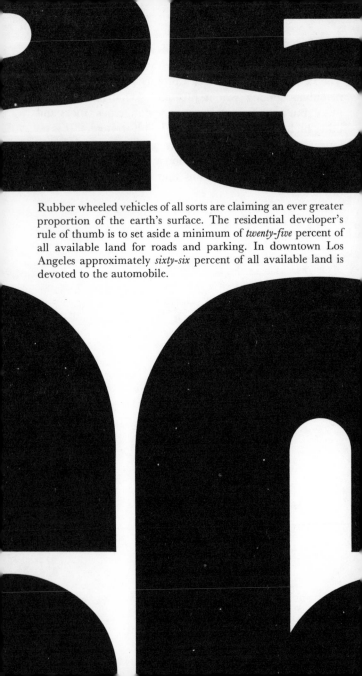

Rubber wheeled vehicles of all sorts are claiming an ever greater proportion of the earth's surface. The residential developer's rule of thumb is to set aside a minimum of *twenty-five* percent of all available land for roads and parking. In downtown Los Angeles approximately *sixty-six* percent of all available land is devoted to the automobile.

7

ENEMY NUMBER TWO: NOISE

There above noise and danger
Sweet Peace sits crown'd with
    smiles.

Henry Vaughan
Peace, *Silex Scintillans*, 1655

Thus noise can have long-winded direct effects. It causes irritation, say, which disturbs sleep. This leads in its turn to high sensitivity and low resilience. Family and business troubles begin, and lead to quarrels which end up by inducing psychological disorders of various kinds. . . . But if the patient manages to move to quieter surroundings, his difficulties usually improve very fast, and the original noise is clearly seen as the source of all the trouble.

Paul Vogler and Erich Kuhn
Medizin und Stadtebau, 1957

Leopold Stokowski, who had halted a recent concert in Philadelphia's Robin Hood Dell when a honking Diesel railroad engine gave the music noisy competition, met even more annoying extra-curricular sound Sunday night at the Lewisohn Stadium where he stopped the concert five times as airliners roared overhead.

New York *Herald Tribune*
August 2, 1960

. . . Whenever possible, in fact, he has a phonograph or radio going, preferably loud. . . . Finding a place to stay that is either without neighbors or with neighbors who will accept Kenton records at top volume at four in the morning is a recurrent problem in his life.

Profile of Mort Sahl
The New Yorker, July 30, 1960

The world is too complex, and living in the world is too hazardous, for any instrument affecting all of us to be allowed to get out of control.

Gilbert Seldes
The Public Arts, 1956

I'm not watching any show. I'm hatching a plot to exterminate your whole miserable industry. (Cartoon of a man disturbed by an opinion-poll telephone call.)

Consumer Reports, September 1960

At the volunteer fire department, we were informed by an untroubled and unshaven man that the siren signified nothing more ominous than the arrival of the noon hour. It was sounded every day, as a sort of public service, and could be heard, our informant told us with pride, for miles.

The New Yorker, August 13, 1960

Human Sanctuary from Noise

Mr. Nevill Long, the timber importer and art collector, has turned part of his 600-acre estate in Bedfordshire into a retreat from noise.

London *Daily Telegraph*

August 31, 1962

ENEMY NUMBER TWO: NOISE

The Look-listen Culture

The tidal wave of radio and television has transformed our lives. Our compulsive submission to the broadcast sound and image surpasses even our capitulation to the car. Ever since the early phonographs and the first telephones, the distant voices of the outside world have been coming more and more insistently into the innermost realms of the house which up till then had been devoted to the familiar sounds and voices of the family.

The dwelling, the vantage point from which we used to look out upon the world before venturing into it, has now become a stage for the venture itself. Transformed by electronics, the dwelling is no longer a refuge but an arena. It now serves as the market place, the forum, the stadium and school, the theater and movie house, rolled into one. Press the button and "you takes yer choice."

Civilized men lead scatterbrained lives: every imaginable reality anywhere around the globe may by some chance become available to the knob twister. If one does not use the immense guide to the offerings on the air and then make a highly specialized selection according to personal interest and taste, one becomes exposed to patterns of events which form a stupendous *non sequitur*.

Triumph of the Vicarious

Television, one of the greatest industries in our economy, has grown in barely a decade from a speculative business into the most powerful instrument of persuasion, seduction, and propaganda known to man. It took even less time to create the "look-listen" culture than the most sanguine of investors in the new technology had hoped. During almost every hour of the day—waking or half-waking—contemporary man is the willing recipient of one message or another, be it information, entertainment, or soporific.

Mankind has developed an insatiable appetite for the half-heard and the barely seen. Even while driving on the turnpike, perhaps one of the few remaining opportunities to be alone and to think, civilized man switches on the radio.

Increased communications are causing most of our experiences to be vicarious. At the push of a button everything is at our command, except the capacity for concentration. The popular use of transistor technology has made it possible, with portable receivers, to keep the "wherever-one-is" in continuous contact with "whatever-else," as if in a desperate attempt to extirpate all possibility of direct experience forever.

The Noise that Came to Dinner

For good or ill, radio and television sets are part and parcel of the Neolithic age of electronics. The quality of sound reproduction and of image projection can only improve. The number of sets, and the number of programs, can only increase. The screens of TV receivers will be larger. Ample screens for the projection of slides and films are already in growing demand. The transformed family album, in full color, is becoming a stock-in-trade of our society. Soon the TV image will be released from the confines of the receiver to share the large screen with the photograph and motion picture. This dramatic enlargement of images of information and entertainment, occurring daily may have some serious consequences; background noise is already competing with conversation, music, and reading; the "life-size" TV image will compete with architecture and works of art. Insulation of various conflicting communications from one another within the house is urgently required.

Acoustic Anarchy

Under present conditions men are beginning to lose the capacity to discriminate between sound and noise—between the desirable and the irrelevant. Some sounds are deliberately selected for their meaning: conversation, the record you are playing, the hiss of a kettle which tells you it is boiling. Other sounds are treated as noise, and deliberately rejected: the millstream, the noise of traffic, the gurgle of the refrigerator. But you can only reject a noise when you are sure enough of what it is to know that you don't want to hear it. There is a huge class of intermediate sounds. These sounds have meaning, but we have not selected them deliberately, and they are only partially heard. These sounds, because we are always straining to understand them, hoping either to select or to reject them, produce a constantly disturbing interference. The most annoying noise is one which is murky, half-clear, or sudden. It is clear enough to represent the possibility of an accident, a criminal, mechanical failure, explosion, or other sinister event. It is unclear enough to remain mysterious and frightening; it does not allow itself to be classified with comfortable familiar sounds.

Yet this kind of background noise is the ever-present obbligato of modern life. This incidental noise, produced by all kinds of domestic equipment, by neighbors, by heavy trucks outdoors, and by distant aircraft, is hard to control —and the farther away the source of noise, the harder. Unable to control it, man adapts to it instead. So far he has managed to remain sane and apparently healthy, but man should give some thought to what may happen to him if the general noise threshold is raised much more.

More Noise Is Less

At close quarters, particularly in crowded offices and dwellings, the situation is acute. The problem of isolating undesirable sounds is technically so hard to solve that acoustics engineers now recommend the simpler expedient of providing artificial background noise in one's own domain as an acoustic cushion or muffler. Making more noise is the only economical way, apparently, of drowning out unwanted noise and of not being overheard. It seems that the illusion of quiet can only be maintained in noise.

What does this process of heaping fire onto ashes do? Since the background noise one was trying to drown out is itself communication (somebody else's), its volume too needs to be raised. Louder and louder the two noise makers scream at one another until everybody and everything is shouting. The artificially created background noise, the "acoustical perfume" that our acousticians prescribe is really not perfume but an acoustical deodorant.

There are probably more serious consequences to all this than mere discomfort or indignity, but the physical and psychological effects have so far been ignored. The noise problem extends beyond the conscious waking hours in man's life. Apparently there is no escape from noise even in sleep. Doctors Volger and Kuhn tell us: "The results of several experiments indicate that it is by no means 'all right' to let children sleep with the noise of traffic or radio in their ears. The quality of sleep they get under such conditions is appalling—and leads inevitably to nervousness, lack of concentration, and all-round vulnerability. For even during sleep acoustic shock causes subconscious reactions which upset the quality and value of sleep."

The form of the human habitat is not designed to accommodate an ever-growing cacophony. Acoustically the habitat is obsolete. The sophisticated organization of the printed TV circuit, for example, is totally unmatched by the organization of the dwelling that contains it.

8

FAITH AND REASON

Cycles of the design process:
historic development from the primitive to the sophisticated.

If there be any principle of structure more plainly inculcated in the works of the Creator than all other, it is the principle of unflinching adaptation of forms to functions.

Horatio Greenough

Form and Function, 1860

Technology is also a unifying force. At one moment there may be several best economic combinations or social arrangements, but only one best technology. The technology can be up to date or antiquated, but there is no question which is which, and the modern is constantly replacing the ancient.

Kerr, Dunlop, Harbison, Myers

Pluralistic Industrialism

Industrialism and Industrial Man, 1960

In an electronic age, all that properly *moves* is information. The massive overlay of antecedent and existent technologies takes on a peculiar character of simultaneity in the electronic age. All technologies become simultaneous, and the new problem becomes one of relevance in stress and selection, rather than of commitment to any one.

Marshall McLuhan

letter from Toronto, 1960

But are we [designers] in a position to seize the opportunities when they arise? Do we have the prestige? Will people heed our advice? Are we high enough in the organization to make our view heard? To all these questions the answer is emphatically, NO. As things are, our status is relatively low, our prestige uncertain and our advice too often rejected. Why? Because of a lack of discipline among ourselves. The status of any profession is reflected in salary scales, fees, social esteem and public respect. On his own subject, the engineer, the lawyer, the surgeon, the banker, the dentist, each is listened to with rapt attention. Why? Because of the training he has undergone? In part; but there is something a great deal more fundamental. Behind the training and behind the professional discipline is a broad agreement on essentials.

. . . The conflict is there. On the one hand, you have the claim of professional discipline. On the other hand, you have the claims of the individual artist. The choice lies before you—the likelihood of being listened to as against the artist's freedom to express himself.

C. Northcote Parkinson

The Corporation and the Designer

Aspen Conference on Design, 1960

Architecture is organization.
YOU ARE AN ORGAN-
IZER, NOT A DRAWING-
BOARD ARTIST.

Le Corbusier

If I Had to Teach You Architecture

Focus, 1938

FAITH AND REASON

The Form Makers

Designed environments will be successful only if they respond to the most crucial pressures of our time. This means that they must resolve the problems created by often useless mobility, the ceaseless sounds and noises of communication and machinery, and the dissolution of the tranquillity and independence known to earlier cultures.

The affluent society chooses to ignore these pressures and bury itself ostrich-like in myths that preserve the illusion of its own comfort and well-being, insensible to the possibility of a disastrous crash. At the same time, it bows to the current absence of independent action, quiet, solitude, and first-hand experience, as if the loss were inevitable, and thereby ignores the potential benefits it is missing. By now, what looks like apathy is often the result of confusion from mere quantity.

The production processes in industrialized society have recently undergone profound changes. But architects and designers remain much the same; no body of specialists in our culture finds it so easy to seek refuge in generalities. None has found it easier to join the busy market-place activity while professing to speak from the forum.

Traditionally, architecture was concerned with the expression of the noblest aspirations of man; it was uniquely the province of artist-scientists. Lately by being forced to include responsibilities for complicated plumbing, it has also become the province of mechanics and includes much broader issues as well. Under the urbanist and architectural umbrellas of our time huddle economists, demographers, housers, traffic experts, builders, structural and production engineers, landscape architects, land-use specialists, lawyers, industrial designers, decorators, and businessmen, as well as artists.

Designer Obsolescence

In futile conservatism, the design schools maintain the tradition of trying to transform average students into universal men of the highest order—to graduate an annual horde of Leonardos. This makes pretentious pseudo artists out of fools and inhibits our best talents because they cannot be conveniently pigeonholed in a conventional manner. Very soon professional schools are likely to have better means of selecting suitable candidates in design than are now employed, and abilities in each class will be more balanced. But the definition of design itself remains ambivalent: is it an art, a profession, a business?

Design schools have become obsolete because they try to perpetuate the traditional image of professional integrity and unique skill personified by the "architect" guiding the "cultured" and unique "client." In truth, both the client and his architect depend largely on the complex and diversified skills and information of many other specialists.

The problem is intensified because the architectural profession, too, as it exists today, is becoming obsolete. And it will continue to be as long as it persists in requiring the schools to serve its immediate, practical purposes. Professional architects and designers require continuity in attitude, in interest, in skills, and in the practice of expediency. Their nature is basically conservative. Design schools, on the other hand, are by definition scholarly, exploratory, adventurous, philosophically long-term minded. Their interest is the exact opposite of the professional's, and their function is to deepen and widen the field as a whole, without exaggerated regard for the immediately practical. Yet it is the professionals who are asked to inspect and accredit schools of architecture from which they draw their assistants and, more often than not, their inspiration.

Pressures and Process

Pressures within the environment change very rapidly and these changes require that the profession adapt itself to the new conditions and reflect the accelerating cycle of obsolescence. K. Lönberg-Holm and C. Theodore Larson have described the life of an object as beginning with the moment when a new problem calls for a new form and ending with the final elimination of the object when it is superseded by one better suited for the job. The cycle has six stages; Research, Design, Production, Distribution, Utilization, and Elimination. A similar diagrammatic statement of the life and death of man-made things by Frederick Kiesler can be seen at the end of Chapter 10. The principle may apply to thought as well as things.

To make systematic thinking serve its proper function in producing form, the known pressures affecting the physical environment will have to be scrutinized at regular intervals and the implications that they have for form constantly re-established by means of organized research.

The analysis of the growth of organic form as a continuous process—a kind of professional service for designers —could be extended to cover any number of characteristic situations. The analyses themselves would be periodically revised and new analyses produced to counteract obsolescence. These analyses would serve a purpose similar to that of engineering data tables which are today in common use.

Manière de Penser

It is noteworthy that our contemporary architectural heroes, Frank Lloyd Wright, Walter Gropius, Mies van der Rohe, Le Corbusier, are as widely admired for their programmatic declarations as for their artistic achievements as form makers. Their cast of thought, their search for what the form wants to be, as Louis Kahn puts it, is often as exciting as the final architectural solution.

Extended and Unified

In the work of great men the statement of the problem becomes an integral part of the process, as important to the design as the physical expression of structure and shape. Lesser, more vulnerable men, who do not have their programs "built in," must cultivate concepts and forge tools to help them cope explicitly with the new needs. Planned decision must replace the ancient process of trial and error. The overwhelming task they face—the shaping of our environment—forces designers to apply themselves to definitions of the human habitat as an extended and unified field for action.

The designer must learn to approach technological changes by taking into account well-known scientific, social, and technical data outside his field that may have an indirect influence upon his work, and he must accustom himself to weighing the largely "invisible" factors that more often than not prove on closer examination to have the most serious implications for physical form.

Form is the ordered expression of a need; the end product of a process of response to pressures. Sometimes the interaction between need, or pressures, and the end product, or form, is direct, immediately clear, and involves relatively simple technology. Under such conditions every form reflects the pressures that are responsible for its existence, and the appropriateness of the form, in terms of its structure and function, may be apprehended accordingly.

Forces have a characteristic pattern, and the good form is in equilibrium with the pattern, almost as though it were lying at the neutral point of a vector field of forces. In contemporary, industrial society simple things exist side by side with those of the greatest complexity. The pattern of pressures changes faster and faster with the drift of culture and the shifts in knowledge and technology. As a result forms easily slip out of equilibrium and become obsolete. The old adage that worked in the craftsman era —that form is the result of individual skill and experience —no longer rings true. It seems equally doubtful that the image of either the artist-architect or the master builder is adequate to a situation that is politically, economically, and technologically highly complex. No end product is better than the program behind it. If the form-making process is obsolete, the design itself will be stillborn.

Design Heuristics

The first step in the process of design, therefore, involves an explicit statement of the forces at work and the pressure pattern the form is to reflect. The designer's task is to create order: to organize conflicting material and to make a form. In our time, even the most gifted and devoted designers find it increasingly difficult to exercise their intelligence and talent at all levels toward this end.

Problems have outgrown a single individual's capacity to handle them. Society must invent ways and means that, in effect, magnify the designer's limited capacity and make it possible for him to apply himself more completely to those problems that he is well equipped to solve. By making the task multistage, he amplifies his capacity to organize in approximately the same way that man magnifies his physical capacity. A single man's strength is limited; but if he needs to do something he is not strong enough to do directly, he can attempt it in stages. For instance, in the first stage he may use his strength to make a lever; he can then in the second stage lift a great weight. The effect of dealing with design problems in several stages, rather than in one fell swoop, is similar.

For this method to succeed, the first stage in architectural design must lie with the problem itself. The most powerful heuristic the designer can find is to state the problem so clearly that the statement itself becomes his lever.

Faith and Reason

Techniques of design, however, cannot serve in lieu of a committed point of view, or faith. This is a point that needs to be stressed in days when it is all too easy to succumb to oversimple scientism. It is not enough for the designer to produce forms with high performance standards. He has a social, technical, and artistic responsibility, and, if necessary, he must be prepared for the sake of these to commit himself to principles not previously tested. A commitment of faith is not less valuable for being a personal commitment or, as it is sometimes termed, a prejudice. Presumably, it is the prejudice of a highly skilled and gifted individual able to sort out the particular aspects of his culture that need to be reflected in form.

Every designer must be so committed in order to be able to identify the frictions and rough edges in his culture that are not yet expressed in existent forms. And only after he has identified them can he begin to discover what implications old and new issues alike may have for design.

Art for Ecology's Sake

The designer's commitment must, however, be a reasoned one that seeks to formulate a more explicit direction for environmental design. The easy devices of pseudo artistry and the "ghastly good taste" of the market place, to use John Betjeman's phrase, have not, it has become evident, been good enough.

The designer's return to his own willful freedom is perhaps a desperate attempt to reassert the humanism that man sometimes seems in danger of losing while he is making gains in science and technology. But in practice, unfortunately, this approach appears to produce little more than decorative shapes that leave the new problems unsolved.

Technology Is a Tool

Designers need to come face to face with the facts of science and technology; their real hope for the restoration of humanism lies in their ability to exploit technique to its limits. The biggest obstacle to improved design standards is the obsolescence of designers themselves. Stubborn refusal to accept the complexity of modern technology and its consequences and to reorganize the design process accordingly is apparent in the chaos of our cities and in the persistently low standards of the majority of contemporary buildings. Monument and doghouse alike bear the dreadful imprint of self-appointed genius or just plain incompetence; and monument and kennel spring up, with equal ease, at the drop of a telephone receiver.

An ever-increasing body of research is providing endless information—facts, figures, specifications—and possibilities which should be reflected in every form. To achieve this end, the designer needs not only to have the data and consultants at his disposal, but to be able to handle them, organize them, bring issues and principles into focus, and make a unified whole out of the many complexities.

But he cannot expect to co-ordinate other disciplines while speaking a private language. In other fields, professionals are respected because, in the long run, they can explain what they are doing. The professional architect usually gets the respect of people outside his special field by relying on mystique and asserting his own genius.

We shall try, in the second part of this book, to deal with the pressing problems of urban form in terms that are clear enough to allow reasonable discussion. Nothing we say calls for respect on the grounds that it is the product of a specialized professional view. Any respect due our suggestions must come from their purpose and efficiency; they are definite enough to be discussed by anyone willing to follow the argument.

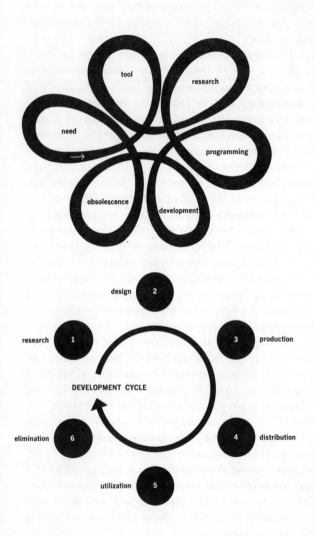

Lower diagram:
development cycle by K. Lönberg-Holm and C. Theodore Larson

PART II: THE URBAN DWELLING

ANATOMY OF URBANISM

General Principles of Organization:
The architecture envisaged in an organism is typical of a pattern which is of wide occurrence not only in the biological but also in the psychological and sociological fields. It can be called *hierarchical order*.

Systems of action, such as the locomotor system consisting of bones, muscles, and nerves, are intelligible only in the way they interact.

Ludwig von Bertalanffy
Problems of Life, 1952

In the coming biotechnic age, as Lewis Mumford has presaged the next to be, criteria to judge design will generally have to be of a well-informed physiological nature.

Richard J. Neutra
The Adaptation of Design to the Metropolis
The Metropolis in Modern Life, 1955

The Plan is the generator.

Without a plan, you have a lack of order, and wilfulness.

The Plan holds in itself the essence of sensation.

The great problems of to-morrow, dictated by collective necessities, put the question of "plan" in a new form.

Modern life demands, and is waiting for, a new kind of plan, both for the house and for the city.

Le Corbusier
Towards a New Architecture, 1924

The Enemies of Urbanity

In Part I we have tried to show that equilibrium in contemporary life is upset by the very features of the environment that give the greatest illusion of comfort and convenience. Civilized man is so accustomed to enjoying the newly discovered benefits of the automobile, broadcasting, and mechanization generally, that the manifold damage they are doing escapes his notice.

The dwelling form must react to the pressures of modern communications media. Yet, as we have shown, the housing designed for the new mobile look-listen society is obsolete. It makes little attempt to solve traffic and acoustic problems and, while supplying the standard, mechanized comforts and conveniences, ignores completely the need for variety in day-to-day life.

Valuable Variety

In ancient times the variety of action required for a well-balanced life was provided by battles for survival alternating with retreats into hiding; today such first-hand excitement has been replaced largely by watching others perform, and restorative rest, by taking sedatives.

It is just possible, of course, that the vastly increased leisure induced by automation will be turned to good account. But as things stand it looks much more as though individual initiative may degenerate still further. Even such skills as those of clerk or miner will vanish with automation to join the other time-honored crafts in limbo.

Variety is already being synthetically produced; it is contrived rather than real. To restore genuine variety each kind of experience must be allowed to develop for itself under conditions that are special, clearly defined, and even physically separate. Without definition and organization experience becomes chaotic, at best incomplete, and inevitably dull.

Such thoughts suggest that in the man-made environment the anatomy of urbanism should be organized at two levels. First, the numberless kinds of experience need to be translated into distinctly articulated and appropriately structured physical zones. Second, these separate zones must be organized in relation to their intensity of effect on each other, in hierarchies, according to their magnitude and quality.

Integrity of Realms

Our first thesis—that every activity be contained in a tangible, physical zone, and that each zone through its formal clarity and integrity induce, reflect, and sustain the activity it has been designed to serve—has long been understood. A few examples will recall its main outline. As long ago as the sixteenth century Leonardo da Vinci proposed in his plans for an ideal city the separation of pedestrians, equestrians and vehicles, and boats, on three different levels. In his 1880 design for Central Park Olmsted foresaw the need for separating different kinds of traffic; pedestrians, equestrians, and vehicles were each given their own channels and integrity in circulation. This same separation of function is also implicit in Tony Garnier's plan for *La Cité Industrielle*, and in the slogan of Patrick Geddes: "Place, folk, work," which was later incorporated into the authoritative 1929 Athens charter of the *Congrès Internationaux de l'Architecture Moderne* (CIAM). The charter describes the need for separating functions and calls for clear organization, within the city, of realms for work, dwelling, recreation, and circulation. This principle of articulation is now generally accepted as a basic tenet of city planning.

None has illustrated the principle of zoned city planning better than Le Corbusier whose prophetic ideas on urbanism have become the inspiration of later designers.

His first full-fledged essay in 1922 produced the plan for *La Ville Radieuse,* in which mobile industrial society living in extremely high densities was first given expression in an exclusively high-rise metropolis.

He was commissioned after the Second World War to make a plan for St. Dié, a modestly dimensioned industrial city that had been almost totally destroyed by German bombing. The plan was never executed, but in it the civic center, residential and industrial areas, and mechanized transportation were given a clear articulation.

For Chandigarh, the capital city of the Punjab now under construction, Le Corbusier further extended in his master plan the definition of the diverse domains of the city and, in particular, the separation of the two major circulatory systems of vehicles and pedestrians.

Hierarchical Organization

Our second thesis—hierarchical organization—is less widely recognized. It is only recently that the expanded spectra of speed and mobility have raised questions in relation to the human scale and suggested the need for an extended hierarchy of relationships between man and his environment.

To this thesis Louis Kahn has contributed the analogy between traffic patterns and the hierarchy: "Rivers, harbors, canals, docks."

Similar attitudes to planning issues may well include hierarchies of new sorts, based not only on extensions of mobility but on the new extension of communications. No doubt other aspects of the environment can also in time be organized hierarchically. We are convinced by the scientific evidence now available that hierarchical organization is an important feature of any complex form, whether natural or technical, and is, therefore, germane to the urban problems of the modern world.

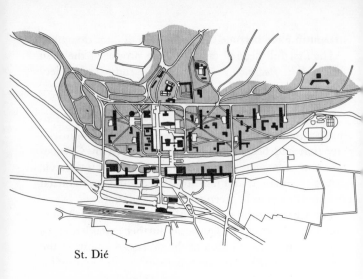

St. Dié

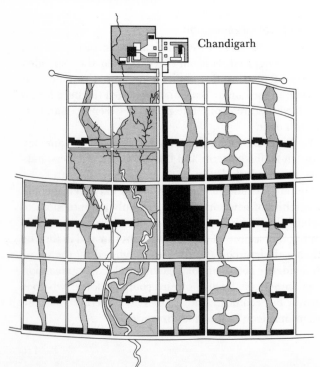

Chandigarh

Six Domains of Urbanity

At this point in the argument it is useful to take the familiar, highly general zoning categories, with the functions and realms associated with them, and break them down still further so that other realms and hierarchies may perhaps become visible.

Our commitment is to those aspects of the articulation of the city that have a direct bearing on privacy. We are interested, principally, in establishing the integrity of those places where the smaller human scales of immediate experience are possible. But the words "space," "zone," and "realm" are abstract and fail to conjure up images of physical actuality, of place, character, or size. Before analyzing the urban anatomy in greater detail, we must describe our commitment in terms that can be translated into social, physical, functionally comprehensible, and easily visualized places.

Roughly speaking the urban hierarchy of spaces or realms for community and privacy fall into six domains.

Urban-Public. The places and facilities in public ownership: highways, roads, paths, civic parks.

Urban-Semi-public. The special areas of public use under government and institutional controls: city halls, courts of justice, public schools, post offices, hospitals, transportation exchanges, parking lots, garages, service stations, stadia, theaters.

Group-Public. The meeting ground between public services and utilities and private property requiring joint access and responsibility: places requiring mail delivery, garbage collection, utilities control, access to fire-fighting equipment or other emergency rescue devices.

Group-Private. Various secondary areas under control of management acting on behalf of private or public interest for the benefit of tenants or other legal occupants: reception, circulation, and service spaces; community gardens; playgrounds; laundries; storage; etc.

Family-Private. The spaces within the private domain controlled by a single family that are devoted to communal family activities such as eating, entertainment, hygiene, and maintenance.

Individual-Private. The "room of one's own," the innermost sanctum to which individuals may withdraw from their family.

This study will be restricted to the residential Group-Private domain, and, within this restriction, only certain components will be discussed in detail. Moreover, since provisions for community living such as parks, playgrounds, and meeting places of all kinds seem to be currently highly prized by city planners, we shall concentrate instead on the relatively neglected aspects of privacy.

Historic Integrity

In cultures both present and past where recognition of the dichotomy or separation of public *and* private has not been overcome by complexities, as it is in modern industrialized society, there is clear physical expression of the need for varying degrees of privacy and the integrity of domains corresponding to these. There are many examples of hierarchical arrangements of space provided by history at many levels of sophistication.

In the Cameroons, the farms of the Mousgoum follow the earlier nomadic camp pattern. Always ready for defense, conical mud huts baked to a ceramic hardness by the sun, are contained within a circular enclosure of the same construction. The compound follows a carefully contrived sequence of increasing privacy from entry to the chief's domain and women's quarters.

The nuraghi are citadels of Sardinia dating from the eighth century B.C. The fortezza d'Orrolli is a perfect example of cumulative security built in three concentric stages: the central tower, later surrounded by a pentagonal fortification, and finally by a larger rough octagonal.

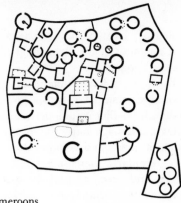

Farm Compound, Cameroons

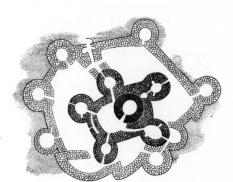

Fortress, Sardinia

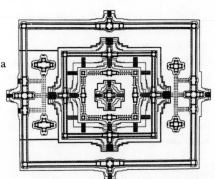

Temple, Cambodia

Rising step by step from the barren hills, the organization and meaning of the stronghold must have been immediately apparent.

Baphuon, a Khner temple of A.D. 1050–1066, is a remarkable example of proportional order, designed to maintain the illusion of a perfect pyramid from the single point of approach across the surrounding moat. The repetition of motifs and volumes from the water level up, in three regularly increasing terraces, is so perfectly conceived and executed that the spectator sees the soaring pyramid immediately on entering in spite of the great horizontal dimensions.

The Buddhist monastery in Peking is a sacred hierarchy. The inner Temple court is itself contained within a park in turn contained within a larger walled park. The pilgrim approaches the great marble altar through a series of calculated spatial events: a sequence of variations on the themes of circle and square, differing in arrangement and dimension, linked by narrow processional paths, terminating in gateways that provide the counterpoint beat of transition points.

The Japanese palace is a direct expression of a plan designed to serve a social hierarchy. The entrance to the princely realm, which is entirely enclosed by a wall, is flanked by grand courts and leads into the first three pavilions for court and ceremonial functions, beyond which lie the two private pavilions of the residence, opening onto a large pleasure garden. The architecture is a beautifully organized hierarchy of structures and complementary outdoor spaces.

The early Renaissance palace at Urbino in Central Italy, built by the second duke, Federigo da Montefeltro, is again organized in three clearly defined zones: the entry complex containing the guards' quarters, the great reception rooms around a central court, and the inner ducal sanctuary protected by a precipice at its back and guarded

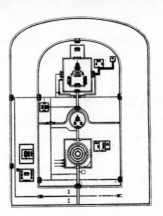

Monastery, China

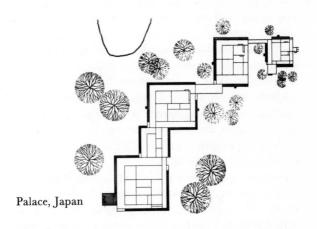

Palace, Japan

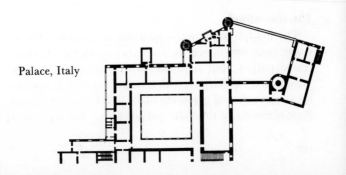

Palace, Italy

in its approaches by links designed for defense. This provides a sequence of three functions: security, ceremony, and privacy.

Modern Space-salad

Most dwellings of our civilization in our time have lost this clarity both in their internal and external organization.

The failures of external organization are in large measure due to an irrational attachment to the country-house ideal which is becoming impossible to attain. The close-packed, freestanding suburban house is an anomaly left over from the time when spacious terrains made it possible for the house to stand really free. Then, the distances between houses offered effective insulation against noise, strangers, and the spread of fire. Today, the space surrounding the suburban house is merely leftover space. It is a wasteful and unproductive anachronism.

The close-packed, pseudo country house is too near the neighbors, acoustically and visually, to make any real seclusion possible. Mandatory setbacks no longer make sense as fire gaps, for greater safety can be ensured by the use of more appropriate means of fire prevention and fire-resistant building materials.

The paltry spaces between houses constitute a nuisance as well as a waste. Side windows, only a few feet removed from the side windows of the neighboring house, are not essential and are little more than embarrassing peepholes and acoustic leaks.

The Non-street

The inappropriateness and waste of the street has already been mentioned in connection with the changing traffic pattern, but it should not be forgotten that the "front yard" which goes with it is also wasteful. It is wasteful as a functioning extension of the street. It is not the outdoor extension of the inner private space that it pretends to be. It is neither public nor private. All that can be said of this random distribution of house and land—dwelling peas on a developer's drum—is that by no possible means can their basic disorder be fitted into a functional hierarchy of the kind we are looking for.

To the inevitable: "But the well kept front yard is so lovely for the passer-by," the obvious answer is that this is not the only way to delight the "passer-by." Among the great visual pleasures of an urban environment are the well-designed walls, fences, and façades of attached houses, like those that make the streets, squares, and terraces in a historic city like Bologna so delightful even for the suburbanite tourist.

The All-too-open Plan

Much of contemporary failure in the internal organization of dwellings stems from reaction against the meanness of the post-Victorian "villa"—originally a most praiseworthy reaction. The structurally obsolete interior walls of the pseudo palace, which had gone on shrinking under pressure of building and land costs, were eliminated. The separate little rooms were replaced by a continuous and visually more generous space.

People are still fascinated by the possibility of illusory spaciousness within modest physical dimensions. The overwhelming majority of architects continue to develop variations on the theme of "exciting space." So visual have Americans become (if we are to believe a thesis supported by the clamor of the *House and Garden*-minded) that Americans have allowed their sense of hearing and the other senses essential to human welfare and pleasure to atrophy.

The conflict between the current image of "visually exciting" open space and the functional specifications for a modern dwelling capable of meeting the demands of the electronic age is obvious. Those who are sharp of hearing and sensitive to interruptions are better off if they live in houses of an earlier structural technology where, as it happens, the separate, insulated rooms are better suited to present-day communications.

We do not question the "pleasure domes" of elegance destined for very special use. The wealthy bachelor who loves chamber music at home, the childless couples who collect works of art or entertain large numbers of guests are not under discussion here. Our point is that this architecture is irrelevant to commonplace family purpose. Cheap eclecticism and the individual follies of developers aided by aesthetic and romantic ingenuities of professional designers have delayed essential rethinking of family-house problems.

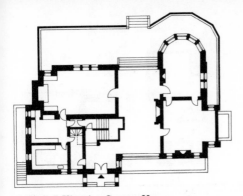

A Typical Victorian Country House
A miniature manor with hallway acting as junction between
service quarters and owner's living rooms on the entry side. The
dining room is similarly placed on the garden side. The study
and one other room are buffered by the formal drawing room
from the rest of the house. The bearing walls around each
"room" give each space the potential of its individual and separate "acoustic climate."

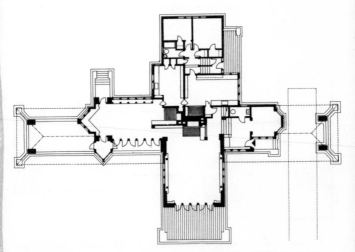

Willet House   *Frank Lloyd Wright, 1902*
The plan retains the separation of the service quarters, but
entry, living, and dining are not rooms but zones in a single
space of changing levels and volumes.

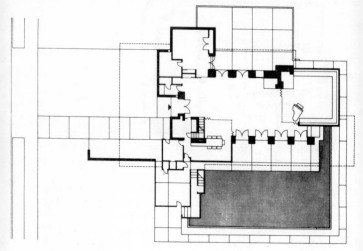

"Life" Family House Project   *Frank Lloyd Wright, 1938*
The ground floor plan is completely open with the kitchen merely placed out of sight. Entry, dining, sitting, recreation, although described as rooms, divisible by sliding screens, are in fact one continuous space with no real separation.

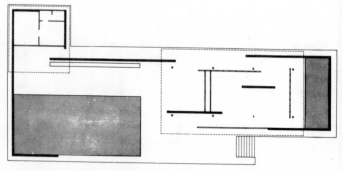

German Pavilion, Barcelona Exhibition   *Mies van der Rohe, 1929*
The first full expression of the continuous space articulated and given direction and flow by freestanding walls. Continuity of space combines with exhibit circulation.

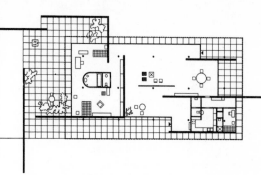

House for the Berlin Exhibition   *Mies van der Rohe, 1931*
The Barcelona principle is applied to a residence. Free walls
define zones and by extending beyond the roof and glass make
indoor and outdoor space into one.

Farnsworth House   *Mies van der Rohe, 1950*
The house designed for a single occupant is virtually an "open"
pavilion. The single enclosed volume of the service core brings
subdivision of the plan to a minimum. The space around the core
radiates beyond the actual enclosure into surrounding landscape and becomes an integral part of the visible environment.

10
WHICH HIERARCHIES

Hierarchies of Urbanism

Hierarchies of Control

Hierarchies of Technology

Hierarchies of Obsolescence

Law and Obsolescence

Hierarchies of Attachment

An organism displays not only a morphological *hierarchy of parts* but also a physiological *hierarchy of processes*. More accurately stated: an organism does not represent one hierarchy that can be described thoroughly in morphological terms. Rather it is a system of hierarchies that are interwoven and overlapping in many ways, and that may or may not correspond to the levels of the morphological hierarchy.

Ludwig von Bertalanffy
Problems of Life, 1952

Hierarchies of Urbanism

It is clear, if the observations in Chapter 8 are accepted as valid, that the dwelling must be considered an organic part of the larger environments. The house is part of the urban anatomy in the way that a vital organ is part of a living creature—for example, the lungs in the mammal—and, like all the other parts of the organism, it is dependent on circulatory and communications systems for its proper function.

This general picture, however, does not indicate the specific properties the particular organ needs. It tells nothing of its size, or how many units there should be. By the same token, the general need for privacy does not in itself determine the characteristics of the different domains, or their size, or how many there should be within the hierarchy. To specify the domains more clearly, hierarchies of control, technology, and obsolescence must be considered.

Hierarchies of Control

For all kinds of control, it is roughly true that the smaller the domain to be controlled, the more controllable it is. Consider, for example, climatic control. Control of weather on the macrocosmic scale is not yet feasible technically, and although it may be in the future it will still be enormously expensive. Even keeping highways clear of snow and flood calls for vast investments of equipment, energy, and manpower. However, as we approach the microcosmic scale, we can afford to do more and more for a reasonable price. Parking spaces of moderate size and pedestrian walks can be cleared manually or mechanically, or the snow even melted by ground warming. Smaller spaces can be entirely enclosed, heated, and air-conditioned.

The same is true of other kinds of control. The provision

of visual privacy is again hardest in a large space and easiest in a small one. On the beach, visual privacy is almost non-existent, unless you count the gymnastics of bathers trying to undress behind a towel. In a house, an interior windowless bathroom leaves its occupant completely unobserved.

Each kind of control has a natural hierarchy associated with it. The extent of control over climate, for example, does not vary smoothly with the size of the domain to be controlled. In other words, although it is roughly true that the larger the domain is, the less controllable it is, there are also places in the hierarchy where control drops very suddenly as the domain gets larger and other places where there is only slight change. The difference between controlling the climate of a two-acre "park" and that of a four-acre "park" is slight. But the difference between controlling climate in a single "room" and in a "house" is much more considerable. Whereas the "room" can be isolated, the "house" is open to all kinds of functional interchange, that make it relatively much less controllable. This is a critical point in the hierarchy of climate control.

If several hierarchies of control all have such critical points at about the same scale, it is very natural to take this scale as the boundary of a physical domain. An obvious example is the room. Many kinds of control over climate, traffic, sound, visual privacy, etc., are much easier to control for one room than for a larger unit containing more functions. The room therefore makes a natural break point in the physical hierarchy; it is a proper unit of control.

In defining such hierarchies, we must be very careful not to be misled by standard ways of thinking about the problem. If we try to define a hierarchy of shelter taking the word in too obvious a way to mean fixed roofed spaces, we shall miss the fact that there are many kinds of portable shelter at different levels of the hierarchy. One kind of portable shelter is clothing; this is controllable, as is the sleeping bag, a kind of portable shelter invented to provide for survival in northern territory. A third kind of portable shelter, offering a different kind of control, is the car, which has attained the refinement and symbolic stature of historic ritualistic attire. The use of these portable shelters, which themselves move in and out of the more static shelters, obviously affects the decision about where the break points in the shelter hierarchy are to be.

Hierarchies of Technology

Another break point in the physical hierarchy of domains will be defined at the level of several dwellings. In one way or another, whether stacked vertically, laid out along streets, or around courts, dwellings are clustered in groups. How many dwellings should a cluster contain?

The answer to this question will be determined largely by the advantages to be had from collective action. Different facilities become optimum at different cluster sizes. Some things work best as autonomous units; a cooking stove, for example. It would be inefficient for even two families to try to share a stove, because they would always be trying to use it at the same time. An automatic washer-dryer, on the other hand, can easily serve more than one family, because whether it is in the laundry room of an apartment block or in the Laundromat around the corner, its use is staggered over several hours of the day, and can serve ten average families. This number of dwellings served efficiently by one washer-dryer unit becomes then a break point at which additional use by a further family shows diminishing returns.

If one asks the same question for a number of different technological determinants, one obtains other numbers of dwellings to make an optimum cluster from the point of view of these different purposes. Heating systems that employ liquid fuel can begin to use more economical crude oil when they serve about twenty dwellings. Again, it becomes efficient to install high velocity air-conditioning when the load is more than 240,000 cubic feet of air—another figure that points to some twenty dwellings. Both these systems are beyond the means of an average family if installed as autonomous units in a single dwelling. Collective installation, which makes them economically feasible, suggests a cluster of twenty dwellings as another break point in the physical hierarchy, because this break point is efficient for several existing technical purposes simultaneously. The hierarchy that ranges from technical autonomy to technical collectivity is closely parallel to the hierarchy that ranges from privacy to community. This is natural, because everyone wants maximum autonomy in the private domain, while communal domains offer the greatest opportunity for collective technical advantage. It will help, therefore, to define the different degrees of autonomy and collectivity required by a technical problem, because this can again help to determine the sizes of consecutive domains.

Garbage, omnipresent and conspicuous, is a convenient example. In our acquisitive society we are perpetually handling canned, bottled, and wrapped commodities, in addition to vast quantities of printed matter. In any street anywhere one cannot but be aware of spilling-over trash cans, which may stand for days on carefully tended walks. This ever-present garbage problem involves both the autonomous individual family and the more collective management and public authority. The public, semi-public, and private domains meet around the trash can.

If the whole problem were clearly seen in terms of hierarchically organized sanitation, appropriate facilities might be distributed among several domains, and the combined advantages of large collective disposal systems and smaller more autonomous chemical and mechanical sub-systems could then solve the problem. This would help considerably in establishing the desirable relative sizes of adjacent domains. But until the whole matter of garbage disposal and reclamation has been solved, the weekly disposal of the four-hundred acres of woodland that go into each issue of the Sunday New York *Times* will continue to overload garbage cans in the most exclusive suburbs.

Hierarchies of Obsolescence

Another thing that helps to determine the exact nature of different domains is the rate at which different technical inventions obsolesce. All technology is susceptible to change and obsolescence, at different rates and for different reasons. No conclusions about the relative sizes of domains that are based on technical considerations have any general or permanent validity.

For example, at present the generally accepted maximum distance between a dwelling and its car is two hundred feet; the farthest one can walk comfortably with a bundle. This defines the radius of the group-public domain. But if the shopping carts already used in supermarkets are put to use in the ordinary residential pedestrian domain, the two hundred foot limit may easily be challenged—one can wheel a cart with comfort much farther—and the radius of the new group-public domain might be three times as large as the old. Thus, under the pressure of technical advances and changing habit, even patterns and distances of pedestrian circulation are susceptible to drastic revision.

In spite of the fact that the precise size of domains is largely ephemeral we can nevertheless design for change by distinguishing different rates of obsolescence. Mechanical equipment wears out rapidly through intensive use and quickly becomes obsolete as a result of research and development. On the other hand, structural elements usually have a very long life without any loss in efficiency. If changing the short-life elements is not to damage the more permanent elements, the two must be physically separated. We can easily imagine a walled domain, for instance, technically simple but very durable, containing mechanical cores of a most sophisticated kind that obsolesce quickly and require periodic replacement. If we can identify several different rates of obsolescence instead of two, the same argument defines a physical hierarchy of elements, nested within one another.

Law and Obsolescence

At the moment we are prevented from establishing any of these hierarchies or break points between domains by the persistence of obsolete building bylaws and zoning ordinances. "Desirable population density" was a concept coined to help slum clearance, but is irrelevant to the general urban problem. Mandatory setbacks from property lines, brick-backing for the walls of public buildings were specifications useful in the situation for which they were designed, but irrelevant in contexts where means of fire protection have changed completely. What these obsolete ordinances and bylaws do is to impose quite arbitrary kinds of articulation on the city, so that the appropriate articulation called for by functional hierarchies cannot be introduced.

Zoning regulations, prescribing what shall go where, are still believed to be a planning panacea. Unfortunately such prescriptions, without reference to a master plan—a long-term commitment to a principle—can do as much harm as obsolete building regulations by burdening a community with long-term commitments to articulations that have only short-term use.

Hierarchies of Attachment

We are in search, here, of articulations that have the most general significance. We shall therefore not try to determine the exact number or precise size of the domains, because these factors depend on the kinds of fluctuation of technology and use that we have described. The life span of man-made things is not unlike that of living organisms. Their different rates of development and decline make differing demands on their environment and in turn produce differing effects upon it. The diagram at the end of this chapter illustrates the life cycle of objects of use produced in industrialized society, with a typical obsolescence rate of some thirty years. Using the same principle, given precise specifications, similar charts of obsolescence rates may be projected for any number of products or situations. If these are in any way connected, the recognition of the effect of their different rates of obsolescence on one another becomes an important part of the planning process. However, there is one problem that obsolescence does not affect, because it is more permanent: the nature of the hierarchy of domains.

Whatever the precise size and number of the domains may be, the individual integrity of each must be preserved, and the hierarchy must be influenced to a great extent by the connections between domains. In other words, the joints between successive and adjacent domains, the extent of their separation, the precise way they are attached to one another, the kind of transition that needs to occur between them, are all matters of vital importance, irrespective of the particular size and number of domains.

Of all these possible problems of connection, we have selected just one to demonstrate how a problem of this kind can be analyzed and to make clear the physical implications the problem has for planning. In Chapter 9 we listed six urban domains, Urban-Public, Urban-Semipublic, Group-Public, Group-Private, Family-Private, and Individual-Private. We shall now examine, in detail, the nature of the physical connection required between the fifth and the third, the vital junction between the residential realm (Family-Private) and the larger environment (Group-Public). This junction would usually be called the *link between the dwelling and the city.*

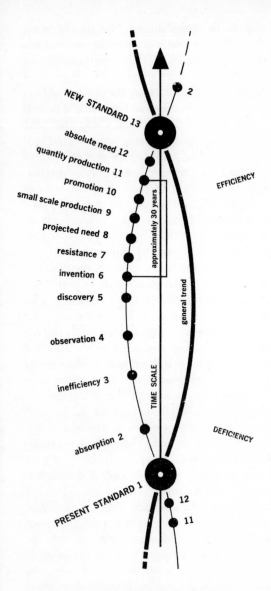

NEW STANDARD 13
absolute need 12
quantity production 11
promotion 10
small scale production 9
projected need 8
resistance 7
invention 6
discovery 5
observation 4
inefficiency 3
absorption 2
PRESENT STANDARD 1

2

12
11

EFFICIENCY

DEFICIENCY

approximately 30 years

general trend

TIME SCALE

diagram: interaction of technology, obsolescence,
and design by Frederick J. Kiesler

11

THE PROBLEM DEFINED

Apparent chaos: the problem unstructured

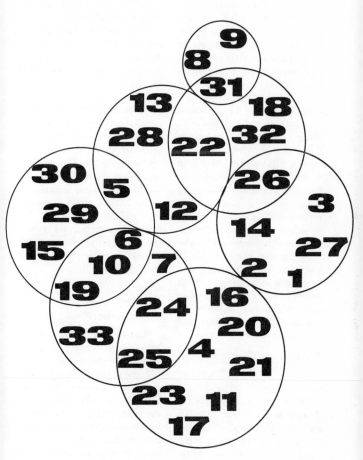

Constellation: the problem structured

Actually, thinking is most mysterious, and by far the greatest light upon it that we have is thrown by the study of language. This study shows that the forms of a person's thoughts are controlled by inexorable laws of pattern of which he is unconscious. These patterns are the unperceived intricate systematizations of his own language — shown readily enough by a candid comparison and contrast with other languages, especially those of a different linguistic family. His thinking itself is in a language — in English, in Sanskrit, in Chinese. And every language is a vast pattern-system, different from others, in which are culturally ordained the forms and categories by which the personality not only communicates, but also analyzes nature, notices or neglects types of relationship and phenomena, channels his reasoning, and builds the house of his consciousness.

Benjamin Lee Whorf
Language, Thought, and Reality, 1956

From 1945 to 1950 was the period of electronic research and the demonstration that machines having many thousand vacuum tubes would indeed operate.

From 1950 to 1955 was the pioneering period in applying computers to the solution of scientific and engineering problems. During the present period, 1955 to 1960, electronic machines are being substituted for clerical effort in commercial organizations.

From 1960 to 1965 we can expect to see the application of digital computers to physical process control. Already there are digital machine-tool controls. . . .

From 1965 to 1970 we should see all these developments converging into pioneering developments in the central management process. The routine, repetitive types of decisions will become more formalized, while management creativeness will be directed to *how* decisions and policies should be made rather than to the actual repetitive making of such decisions.

Jay W. Forrester
Industrial Dynamics
Harvard Business Review, 1958

Rules of structure should not be regarded as more than useful working assumptions which become reliable only when one can specify where they fail. But they provide glimpses of the vistas which will be opened by a science of form. They may develop into the axioms of a way of thinking which will reveal the parallels between all realms in which structure is at work.

It is for mathematical logic

and exact science to clarify these rules and to establish an elegant philosophy of form easy upon the understanding.

Lancelot Law Whyte

Invisible Structure

Accent on Form: An Anticipation of the Science of Tomorrow, 1954

Let us go now to the specimen problem: the attachment of a group of dwellings to the city. By selecting this problem we are involved both with the anatomy of the urban structure as a whole and with the anatomy of dwellings: the way the houses within the city should stand in relation to one another and to the whole—the way two components of an urban form might hang together.

Semantic Hurdles

In view of the conceptual changes that are taking place it is hardly helpful to continue using in connection with housing problems words that are firmly anchored in the cultures of days gone by; they can only mislead us in our present search for better solutions. "Apartments," "row houses," "single-family houses," "yard," "garden," "garbage," "parking lot," "living room," "kitchen," "dining room," "bedroom," "bathroom," are all heavily loaded words that make any number of irrelevant images spring to mind. Designer and user alike may imagine that these words stand for something immutable, though in fact they are just names for the familiar.

Until one stops using popular or generalized words to describe specific objects and events, one will continue to be deceived by the associations with them and will fail to arrive at the essential functional aspect of things and places that is the planner's actual concern in problem-analysis and design.

"Form Follows Function"

Designers do not, on the whole, examine familiar things critically in respect to proper function but only in respect to shape—it requires less effort. To escape from fake traditional and pseudo-modern shapes alike even serious designers feel moved to invent new shapes and new catch-

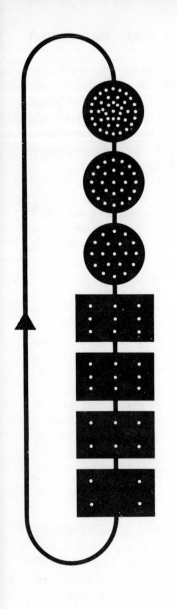

Schematic diagram of the process of abstracting.

by A. Korzybski and Wendell Johnson

submicroscopic

microscopic

macroscopic

label or description

inference 1

inference 2

inference 3 etc.

Four levels represent verbal abstraction of the first order, to which are added levels of increasing generality of statement; inference levels of abstraction. There is of course no "higher" or "lower" level. Each is a step in a continuous process, and the diagram may be read in any direction. Semantic blockage may be represented by a short circuit.

words for each client. Yet the catchwords of "progressivism" are no better than the catchwords of "tradition." If we are to destroy the myths and images that interfere with our clear view of the problem, we must break the problem down into its tiniest, most clearly visible parts and describe these with words that are emotionally neutral; we can then proceed to reassemble them according to the problem's real and proper structure.

Too many designers miss the fact that the new issues which legitimately demand new forms are there, if the pattern of the problem could only be seen as it is and not as the bromide image conveniently at hand in the catalogue, or magazine around the corner.

Anatomy of the Obvious

To see how clear restatement of things usually taken for granted clarifies design problems, let us look at a familiar commonplace. A characteristic junction between outdoors and indoors in house design is fenestration.

It is better for our purpose not to speak of windows. Different experience will conjure up a different "window." It may be a double-hung, vertically sliding, wood window of small panes of glass, dating from the eighteenth century, flanked by louver shutters or even smaller pieces of earlier, lead framed, translucent glass. It may be a modern casement of thin steel frame containing a single piece of glass of extraordinary clearness dimmed a trifle by the insect screen. It may be the sliding door window of great size glazed with heavy plate glass, or the panoramic, single, large, fixed sheet—the familiar and abused "picture window," sometimes framing nothing.

If one's memory is precise all these "windows" and many others will appear in their full panoply of pelmet and drape, curtain, shade, venetian blind, or what have you, and each curtain will be memorable not for its functional but its decorative effects—its texture or the color of the flower pattern. That is all.

If, however, we speak of a sheltering envelope, or an enclosing membrane, which may transmit air, permit light to pass through it, modulate the light, screen it, diffuse it, prevent glare, permit or prevent the passage of living organisms, facilitate control of radiation and of temperature, and prevent transmission of sound or prevent the embarrassing surprises of artificial illumination, something tangible can emerge. In other words "window" does not describe the problem of designing a functioning fenestration system. Only careful examination of obvious needs and disregard for the word "window" makes it possible to recast the problem.

A House by Any Other Name

The process of redefinition and search for a vocabulary capable of describing the infinite variety of elements, situations, activities, or events that make up the complex organism "house" was started by Chermayeff in 1952 in a seminar on environmental design at Harvard University. A supplementary précis was made for a radio broadcast in 1956. In 1959, these original listings were revised and extended in anticipation of the present project. In 1960, with Alexander, the lists were again reworded and further broken down so that they could be related to the question of community and privacy. These lists have served to trigger the analytic process; they cover a great deal of ground. Even in the latest revision, however, they are still imprecisely structured, still bear no exact relation to the structure of the problem. Useful though they are, they contain items of too many different logical types.

Problems Have Patterns

There is an important working principle to note at the outset: Every problem has a structural pattern of its own.

Good design depends on the designer's ability to act according to this structure and not to run arbitrarily counter to it. The standard ways of stating a problem often cut across the pattern and destroy it. To avoid the danger of running counter to the pattern, let us look only at the familiar, well-known aspects of the house and its attachment to the city, selecting only those requirements that are specific, are not obscured by semantic misapprehension, that can be precisely described, that will be recognized as functional commonplaces of our day-to-day lives, and are not a matter of taste.

It is not possible to list, *ad hoc,* all the minute require ments that make up the problem. They are too numerous and too detailed for us to find them without a way of awakening our memories. We therefore attack our specific problem, *the attachment of the public and private domains,* by using the nine functional categories below as key words. The important thing about these categories is that they should, as far as possible, avoid confusing simple issues by conjuring up vivid or irrelevant images. They are convenient pigeonholes for the preliminary sorting of commonplace issues.

Accommodation and Land Use: Spaces for group occupancy.

Problems of Protection: Security devices from society, safety from accidents, immunity from infestation and pollution.

Responsibility: the question of ownership and maintenance, who does what, involving clarity of boundaries.

Climatic Control: how much and what may be controlled to make the entry comfortable as a link between the climatically controlled automobile or public vehicle and the climatically controlled dwelling itself.

Illumination: good visibility in relation to all questions of both safety and pleasure, day and night.

Acoustics: Transition and insulation from the noise environment of traffic through the progressively reduced background noise to the set of semi-private, private, innermost privacy realms.

Circulation: as this relates to the transition between mechanized vehicles, non-mechanized vehicles and the pedestrian himself.

Communication: long-distance communication between the first entry point of the cluster and the final entry point into an individual dwelling, for the purposes of convenience and security at both points.

Equipment and Utilities: adequate accommodation and access to be provided by public authority or by management or by individual owners or tenants in the semi-private "no man's land" of entry zone.

It must be emphasized again that these categories do not in themselves elucidate the structure or pattern of the problem. What they do, by being emotionally neutral, is to help us enumerate at the next stage more precise requirements called for by the need for privacy. Under these headings we can go on to look for detailed pressures that would affect the plan.

Basic Requirements

1 *Efficient parking for owners and visitors; adequate maneuver space.*

2 *Temporary space for service and delivery vehicles.*

3 *Reception point to group. Sheltered delivery and waiting. Provision for information; mail, parcel, and delivery boxes; and storage of parcel carts.*

4 *Provision of space for maintenance and control of public utilities. Telephone, electricity, main water, sewerage, district heating, gas, air conditioning, incinerators.*

5 *Rest and conversation space. Children's play and supervision.*

6 *Private entry to dwelling, protected arrival, sheltered standing space, filter against carried dirt.*

7   *Congenial and ample private meeting space; washing facilities; storage for outdoor clothes and portable and wheeled objects.*

8   *Filters against smells, viruses, bacteria, dirt. Screens against flying insects, wind-blown dust, litter, soot, garbage.*

9   *Stops against crawling and climbing insects, vermin, reptiles, birds, mammals.*

10 *A one-way view of arriving visitors; a one-way visible access space.*

11 *Access points that can be securely barred.*

12 *Separation of children and pets from vehicles.*

13 *Separation of moving pedestrians from moving vehicles.*

14 *Protection of drivers during their transition between fast-moving traffic and the pedestrian world.*

15 *Arrangements to keep access clear of weather interference: overheating, wind, puddles, ice and snow.*

16 *Fire barriers.*

17 *Clear boundaries within the semi-private domain. Neighbor to neighbor; tenant to management.*

18 *Clear boundaries between the semi-private domain and the public domain.*

19 *Maintenance of adequate illumination, and absence of abrupt contrast.*

20 *Control at source of noises produced by servicing trucks, cars, and machinery.*

21 *Control at source of noises generated in the communal domain.*

22 *Arrangements to protect the dwelling from urban noise.*

23 *Arrangements to reduce urban background noise in the communal pedestrian domain.*

24 *Arrangements to protect the dwelling from local noise.*

25 *Arrangements to protect outdoor spaces from noise generated in nearby outdoor spaces.*

26 *Provision for unimpeded vehicular access at peak hours.*

27 *Provision for emergency access and escape, fire, ambulance, reconstruction, and repairs.*

28 *Pedestrian access from automobile to dwelling involving minimum possible distance and fatigue.*

29 *Pedestrian circulation without dangerous or confusing discontinuities in level or direction.*

30 *Safe and pleasant walking and wheeling surfaces.*

31 *Garbage collection point enclosed to prevent pollution of environment.*

32 *Efficient organization of service intake and distribution.*

33 *Partial weather control between automobile and dwelling.*

This list of thirty-three detailed pressures is an extremely obvious one. No item on it is in itself surprising. Every house designer or house occupant knows that each one of these requirements, ideally, should be reflected in the form of the connection between dwellings and city.

Pressures Interact

But the thirty-three requirements do not in themselves constitute the problem. It is true that the task is to find a form that reflects each of the requirements, but the problem is only half defined by them. Before we can grasp the problem fully, we must look at the links that bind the problem, for it is only these links that give it any pattern or internal logic.

This second half of the statement of the problem, as crucial as the first half, is shown diagrammatically. A black dot indicates that two requirements are linked, a clear intersection of lines that they are not.

Each link or absence of a link is a statement about the interaction between the two issues concerned. If what we can do physically about accommodating one issue in the form inevitably affects what we can do about the other (whether positively or negatively), we call them linked. If there is no such interaction, we call them independent.

Analysis of Interaction

Sometimes a link is obvious—like that between 15 and 33 for instance (arrangements . . . partial control). Obviously the provision of one reinforces the provision of the other. Or that between 11 and 27 (access control . . . emergency access) where the provision of one makes the provision of the other more difficult. It is important to notice that a link refers only to functional interaction, not to connections such as habit or vocabulary seem to indicate.

Let us take item 11: The provision of access points that can be controlled. On the face of it, it looks as though this might be connected with, for instance, item 6 (private entry to dwelling), since both are concerned with physical closure. But the provision of a closing device that can be controlled does not effectively inhibit or facilitate provision of an entry. On the other hand, though 11 seems to have little to do with acoustics, if one thinks in terms of physical implications, such as the weight and size and tight fit of a door, one sees the reason for a link between 11, controlled access, and 21, the control of noise. Of course the fact that the entry or access has to be controlled is in itself irrelevant to acoustic considerations. But if access is to be of such a kind that it may be totally closed, this suggests that the closure must be tight, a quality that together with the relatively small dimensions of opening and simplicity of operation does in fact make acoustic as well as climatic control easier.

There will be little disagreement over the statement of these obvious interactions, for it stems from the common body of knowledge available to anyone familiar with the cultural and technical context. Every judgment is based quite simply on experience of the technology available, and on the physical possibilities of planning within the particular context, which happens in this instance to be the highly industrialized urban society of the West.

We are not trying to make the interactions seem startling in themselves. It is rather the pattern they give the problem when they are all taken together that makes them vitally important. Once one has this pattern, in the

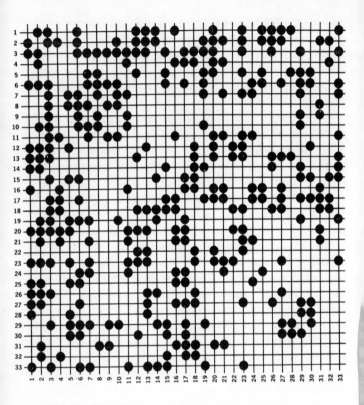

Diagram of interaction between
the thirty-three requirements of the problem

form described, one can proceed to analyze it and to use it.

When a designer is faced with a complicated problem, he looks first at one part, then at another, searching for the various aspects that deserve consideration. Which parts of the problem are going to be most useful? His desire is to select those that will guide him most surely toward a competent solution.

The Crucial Question

The numberless interactions between the various individual items of the list make it impossible to consider all the items at once. Therefore, since they have to be considered group by group, the next question is to determine which groups of items should be taken together.

This is the crucial question in any design process, for countless different views of the problem are possible. The most fruitful aspects to consider, can we but identify them, are those most deeply related to the structure of the problem. The sense in which the structure given by the grouping of parts can help us solve a problem is illustrated beautifully in the words Chuangtzu, who lived at the time of Plato, put into the mouth of a Taoist butcher:

"A good cook changes his chopper once a year—because he cuts. An ordinary cook, once a month, because he hacks. But I have had this chopper nineteen years, and although I have cut up many thousand bullocks, its edge is as if fresh from the whetstone. For at the joints there are always interstices, and the edge of a chopper being without thickness, it remains only to insert that which is without thickness into such an interstice. By this means the interstice will be enlarged, and the blade will find plenty of room."

If the pieces of the problem selected for consideration are arbitrarily chosen, there is no guarantee that they will merit independent treatment. Indeed, if the parts the designer chooses to consider cut across the structure of the problem, the result of his consideration will be blunt and ineffectual, like the unskilled butcher's treatment of the bullock. The problem must be split apart at its interstices. Most parts of the problem are so closely linked to other parts that it serves no purpose to consider them alone. We must try to find parts with so much integrity that they can be considered as isolated units.

The integrity of a problem can be thought of as the counterpart to the natural pieces of the bullock described by the Taoist butcher. Provided we can identify the cleavages inherent in the structure of the problem, we can identify those parts of the problem with the greatest integrity.

Ten Billion Joints

The problem as it stands is immensely complex, far too complex to be grasped "by eye." The selection of such cleavages, even in a structure that contains only thirty pressures, involves the successive comparison of some 10,000,000,000 different cleavages—a task well beyond the capacity of man, even though the problem is a comparatively small one.

The Computer Comes In

Problems of this kind cannot be solved without the help of electronic computers. But let us be very clear about the part computers play in the analysis. The machine is distinctly complementary to and not a substitute for man's creative talent. Man is able to invent relations between things, and to see things in a new framework, but in any complex situation he is unable to explore the relations very deeply without prohibitive expense of time. The computer, while unable to invent, can explore relations very quickly and systematically, according to prescribed rules. It functions as a natural extension of man's analytical ability.

Design today has reached the stage where sheer inventiveness can no longer sustain it. To make adequate forms, one must be able to explore the relations between circumstances more fully than is done at present, so that the decision as to just where to apply precious and limited inventive power can be made. Fortunately, large computers and the techniques for data-processing have become generally available in the past decades.

The IBM 704 computer at The Massachusetts Institute of Technology, given the appropriate instructions, found the major cleavages for our attachment problem in a few minutes. A galaxy on closer scrutiny is seen to be composed of stellar systems. The collection of thirty-three items given on our list is similarly arranged: apparent chaos is resolved into coherent groupings. The resolution of the apparent chaos of thirty-three items into groupings is made clear in the diagram introducing and closing this chapter.

Diagrams and Plan

Our particular problem has some seven principal components. Of these seven components two, A and D, have no implications for plan but would primarily affect the materials used and the mechanics of control.

Since plans are the primary concern here, we considered in detail only the remaining five problem components, B, C, E, F, G. For each one we worked out a diagram that attempts to reveal the full implications of that component for the plan of the dwelling cluster. The diagrams are presented with an explanation of the issues they contain.

It must be emphasized that these diagrams are not mere illustrations or accompaniments to the text. They are hard won, carefully worked out schematic statements that summarize (visually) the physical implications of the various components of the problems. In working them out we went through all the familiar difficulties of solving planning problems except that since these component problems were of manageable size we were more certain that most of the possibilities were explored.

There are special difficulties associated with the formation of such diagrams. It is very difficult to explore the full implications of a component problem without introducing arbitrary and irrelevant external suppositions. We have tried to make each diagram not only solve the component problem as specifically defined by its requirements and their juxtaposition, but also achieve a level of generality that makes it clear that the diagram contains no extraneous assumptions.

This dual pupose—total specificity as regards the requirements under discussion, and complete generality as regards pressures not under immediate discussion—is extremely hard to achieve. It is in fact the critical part of the preliminary stages of the design process where the program for action is first developed.

Component A

5 *Rest and conversation space. Children's play and supervision.*

6 *Private entry to dwelling, protected arrival, sheltered standing space, filter against carried dirt.*

10 *A one-way view of arriving visitors; a one-way visible access space.*

15 *Arrangements to keep access clear of puddles, ice, and snow.*

19 *Maintenance of adequate illumination, and absence of abrupt contrast.*

29 *Pedestrian circulation without dangerous or confusing discontinuities in level or direction.*

30 *Safe and pleasant walking and wheeling surfaces.*

Component D

8 *Filters against smells, viruses, bacteria, dirt. Screens against flying insects, wind-blown dust, litter, soot, garbage.*

9 *Stops against crawling and climbing insects, vermin, reptiles, birds, mammals.*

31 *Garbage collection point enclosed to prevent pollution of environment.*

We have no diagrams for these two, since they primarily affect materials and mechanics.

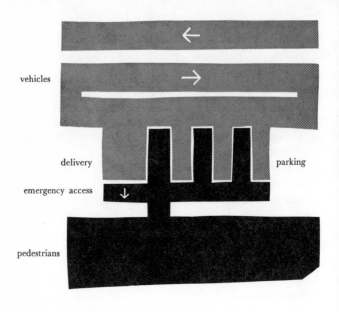

Component B

1 *Efficient parking for owners and visitors; adequate maneuver space.*

2 *Temporary space for service and delivery vehicles.*

3 *Reception point to group. Sheltered delivery and waiting. Provision for information; mail, parcel, and delivery boxes; and storage of parcel carts.*

14 *Protection of drivers during their transition between fast-moving traffic and the pedestrian world.*

26 *Provision for unimpeded vehicular access at peak hours.*

27 *Provision for emergency access and escape, fire, ambulance, reconstruction, and repairs.*

Analysis B

26 and 14 call for smooth one-way traffic flow, alongside and parallel to the traffic artery that must itself be one-way. Right-angle access would be dangerous. Entry and exit are separated to avoid bottlenecks.

14 cannot allow incoming traffic to cut between pedestrians and parking spaces. So that each car may have its own protected pedestrian access, pedestrian and parking domains cannot simply abut, but need to interlock.

1 and 2 call for separation between private vehicles and public ones. This articulation also simplifies the solution of 3, since the reception point needs to be approached from one side by the dwellers and from the other side by the delivery men.

Emergency access, 27, must always be free, yet will almost never be in use as such. To avoid wasting space, we double it up with the only used space that is guaranteed free—the unloading zone called for by 2 and 3 (drivers of delivery vehicles are always on hand to move their trucks).

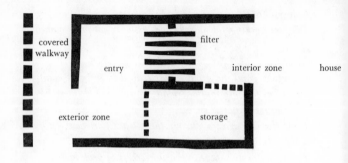

Component C

6 *Private entry to dwelling, protected arrival, sheltered standing space, filter against carried dirt.*

7 *Congenial and ample private meeting space; washing facilities; storage for outdoor clothes and portable and wheeled objects.*

10 *A one-way view of arriving visitors; a one-way visible access space.*

19 *Maintenance of adequate illumination, and absence of abrupt contrast.*

24 *Arrangements to protect the dwelling from local noise.*

25 *Arrangement to protect outdoor spaces from noise generated in nearby outdoor spaces.*

33 *Partial weather control between automobile and dwelling.*

Analysis C

6 and 7 call for a pair of zones, 6 for a separating filter.

10 and 19 put the entrance to the exterior zone and the closing devices leading to the interior zone in line with one another—to provide visibility.

24 calls for wing walls to protect the exterior zone from local noise, and also for a baffle to protect the actual point of access from the noise of local circulation; 25 again calls for surrounding walls and for small exterior space.

33 doubles up with 25 in calling for cover, which is extended beyond the exterior private space as far into the pedestrian domain as possible. Screen walls, 24 and 25, also act as weather insulators against wind and sun.

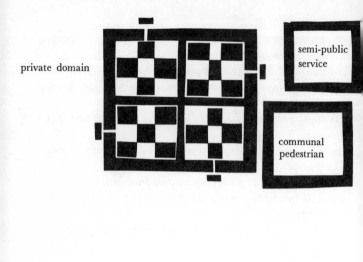

private domain

semi-public service

communal pedestrian

Component E

4 *Provision of space for maintenance and control of public utilities. Telephone, electricity, main water, sewerage, district heating, gas, air conditioning, incinerators.*

11 *Access points that can be securely barred.*

16 *Fire barriers.*

17 *Clear boundaries within the semi-private domain. Neighbor to neighbor; tenant to management.*

20 *Control at source of noises produced by servicing trucks, cars, and machinery.*

21 *Control at source of noises generated in the communal domain.*

23 *Arrangements to reduce urban background noise in the communal pedestrian domain.*

24 *Arrangements to protect the dwelling from local noise.*

25 *Arrangements to protect outdoor spaces from noise generated in nearby outdoor spaces.*

Analysis E

4 and 17 call for three distinct zones, the private, the communal pedestrian, and the semi-public service.

11, 16, 20, 21 call for barriers surrounding these three domains, and 23 and 24 call for buffers between domains.

24 and 25 can only be answered if all of the private outdoor spaces are very small with high walls, preferably not adjacent but always separated by roofed spaces. This leads to the high fragmented indoor-outdoor space shown in the diagram.

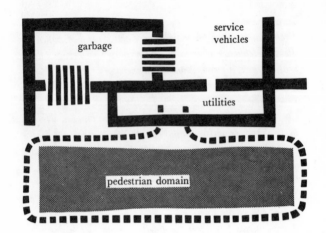

Component F

18 Clear boundaries between the semi-private domain and the public domain.

22 Arrangements to protect the dwelling from urban noise.

26 Provision for unimpeded vehicular access at peak hours.

31 Garbage collection point enclosed to prevent pollution of environment.

32 Efficient organization of service intake and distribution.

Analysis F

The clear boundary between the service zone and the pedestrian domain, called for by 18, is most easily achieved if they share only one edge.

If the service zone is also placed next to the traffic artery, then it allows clear vehicular access and satisfies requirement 26. Since its use is intermittent, it need only have minimal drawoff space.

The location of this pair of zones doubles up with 22, which calls for a buffer between the pedestrian world and vehicular noise.

This buffer becomes still more effective if the quiet service distribution (which is best linear for the sake of clarity, 32) itself separates the pedestrians from the noisy garbage area. To avoid pollution and irritation, garbage entry is withdrawn from major pedestrian circulation, 31.

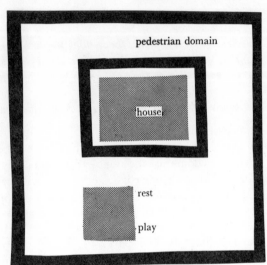

Component G

5   *Rest and conversion space. Children's play and supervision.*
12 *Separation of children and pets from vehicles.*
13 *Separation of moving pedestrians from moving vehicles.*
22 *Arrangements to protect the dwelling from urban noise.*
28 *Pedestrian access from automobile to dwelling involving minimum possible distance and fatigue.*

Analysis G

These items at first seem strange and unrelated. The solution becomes clear when we see that the pedestrian circulation space called for by 28 can double up for 22 by acting as a buffer (of intermediate noise level) between the quiet house and the surrounding urban noise.

This buffer space is made effective by being sandwiched like air in a cavity wall between barriers called for both around the dwelling, 12, and between the pedestrian domain and traffic, 13.

Children's play, 5, and space for rest, conversation, and other activities of the group can be located within the buffer, as far as possible from automobile access.

Composite Diagram

Following the development of these five diagrams, our next step was to put them together. The composite diagram opposite is a translation of these five diagrams into a possible plan.

The basic component of the plan is the cluster of dwellings, its size determined by technical considerations; we have assumed this will turn out to be about twenty dwellings.

The inner nature of the cluster is a highly fragmented pattern of open and closed space, as given by E. This is achieved by many-court dwellings, arranged so that each court abuts only closed rooms, never another court. The pattern offers maximum privacy and acoustic protection, and yet permits high density.

Each cluster is surrounded by pedestrian circulation which, as in G, buffers it to some extent from the noise of traffic beyond. The dwelling opens on this public pedestrian surround, through its entrance lock C. By adopting a pin-wheel arrangement for the cluster as a whole, these locks C can be placed so that front doors of houses in adjacent clusters do not open into one another's faces.

The composite clusters with their surrounding circulation are separated from vehicular traffic by a solid wall of alternating transfer points B, and service zones F, each substantial enough as a building to provide further separation and acoustic protection. The capacity of these components B and F is worked out so that each cluster is served by one B and one F.

The organization of this composite plan is hierarchical. The hierarchy is maintained by isolating domains from one another, and by providing for the transfer between domains.

Physical ideas of transfer and separation were already present cloudily in the recognition of cultural pressures demanding privacy. The purpose of the analysis has been to make clear the relation between this commitment to the search for privacy and the specific components of urban form to which the commitment leads. The structure of the problem has been organized to the point where its implications for physical form begin to be clear.

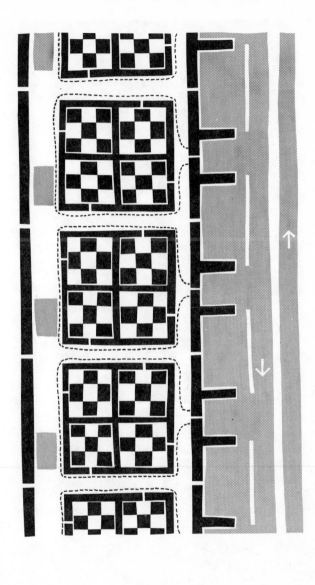

Constellation: the problem structured

12
CRITICAL APPRAISAL

Stereotype Clusters

The Search for a Form

Principle Applied

Houses are built to live in, and not to look on: Therefore let use be preferred before Uniformity, except where both may be had.

Francis Bacon
Of Building, 1612

Too many stairs and back doors make thieves and whores.

Sir Balthazar Gerbier
Counsel and Advice to All Builders, 1663

The plenty and cheapness of good land are such powerful causes of prosperity, that the very worst government is scarce capable of checking altogether the efficacy of their operation.

Adam Smith
The Wealth of Nations, 1776

Then in a short, incredibly short, time, we, and still more they, shall have these dwellings, and with them the substantial and assured, the wholesome and delightful, contribution to the sustenance of their inhabitants which gardens, properly understood and worked, imply.

Patrick Geddes
Paleotechnic and Neotechnic
Cities in Evolution, 1913

Most of the land shortage talk you hear is nonsense. . . . The easiest-to-build-on big acreage of flat land just the right distance out in the right direction may be gone, but there are millions of acres of by-passed land closer to town than most of today's new tracts, more millions of acres of by-passed land than the housing industry will need for many, many years. . . .

Ernest Fisher and Mason Gaffney
House and Home
Current, October 1960

CRITICAL APPRAISAL

Stereotype Clusters

Armed with our newly found principle we can now go one step further and examine some existing stereotypes to see whether they contain the five plan-generating components our analysis suggests.

The family houses that follow have been selected because they fall readily into a few recognizable and characteristic types:

The Suburban Developer's Subdivision and picturesque *variations* on this by architects and others. Here land distribution and use is concerned only with roads and lots. To all intents and purposes the components are planless.

The Garden City. Pioneered in England, the green-setting ideal reached its second stage of development in America where the ubiquitous car had to be accommodated and called for some separation of pedestrians and vehicles.

The Functional Order. This combination of logical planning, characteristic of German thought, and French *urbanism* as a concept of urban order was developed by the *Congrès Internationaux de l'Architecture Moderne* (CIAM) led by Le Corbusier in France and Gropius in Germany.

The Court House Cluster. Still part of work in progress, this is merely one variant of many proposals that are an extension of the CIAM principle. The tight grouping of family houses enables them to share communal facilities and amenities not available in earlier projects and makes these houses virtually *Apartments on the Ground* with the additional inestimable advantage of private outdoor living.

At densities of approximately fifty persons per acre, family houses on the ground become practical in urban housing near city centers and, with a reasonable proportion of apartment housing of varying heights, no reduction of over-all desired densities for residential sectors in urban areas need occur.

The quantities given in each case—square-foot area of individual property, number of houses in the group, and number of persons per acre—are rough estimates. Obviously, these quantities may vary from place to place in accordance with site conditions.

The Search for a Form

Our composite cluster diagram gives some indication of the organization required. It will be seen that many particulars have already been recognized and at least partially expressed in form by other designers. Yet many plans that at first sight appear to be good are, in fact, failures, because they lack an appropriate programmatic base and conflict, in our view, with the most vital requirements of the situation.

Principle Applied

The house clusters examined here may, of course, have been constructed of materials, or employed control methods, completely unsuited to meet the standards prescribed. These we will ignore. We have purposely chosen plans in which differences in structural and mechanical factors are irrelevant. Any one of them can be constructed and equipped in diverse ways, provided the program is adequate.

We are looking at the house clusters from the point of view of plan organization, and not for structural or mechanical specifications, or aesthetic values. Different technical and economic possibilities, or special attitudes of designers, in no way affect the underlying tenets.

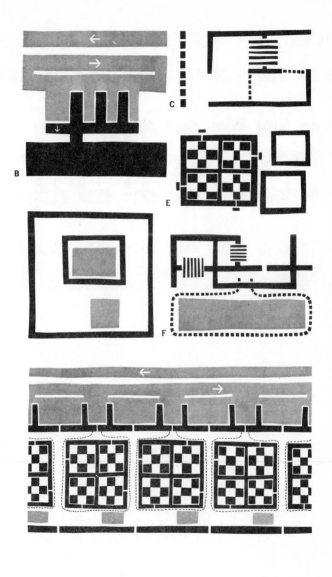

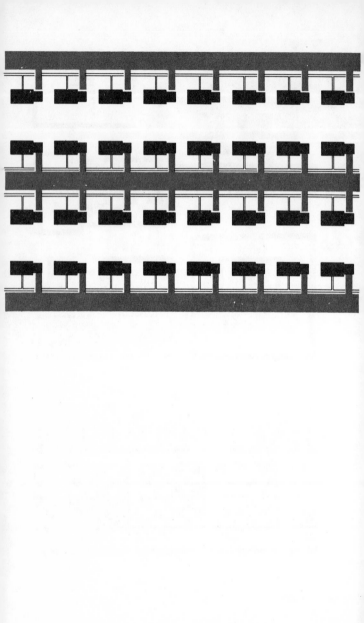

1 *Typical Suburban Subdivision*
5000 square feet/house   4 houses/acre   14 persons/acre

Critique

B Owners back their cars onto the street across pedestrian walks. Visitors' cars and delivery trucks have to park in the street.

C Each house entry is open to the street and has neither physical security nor climatic, hygienic, or acoustic protection.

E Servicing is in the street, and not separated from traffic and access. There are no acoustic buffers between street and house, or between neighbors.

F Maintenance responsibility is not clearly defined, so that street and sidewalks invite neglect. Garbage disposal is a special nuisance.

G No safe private outdoor space. Perpetual conflict between traffic, pedestrians, and children's play. The minimal distance between car and house (where you find parking space) is bought at a great price.

Conclusion

This typical arrangement of separate-lot, single family houses produces mostly unusable space, and fails in all particulars.

2 *Suburban Subdivision   Students in the Yale School of Architecture*
10 houses/cluster   3500 sq. ft./house   5 houses/acre
18 persons/acre

Critique

B Parking areas form a transition zone.

C No security, visual privacy, hygienic or acoustic protection.

E No acoustic buffers between the street and the house, or between neighboring houses.

F The peace of the entire cluster is disrupted by any major servicing activity. The cluster's semi-private parking area is very susceptible to poor maintenance.

G Conflict between traffic, pedestrians, and children at play. No private outdoor space. No modification of urban noise in the available outdoor space.

Conclusion

The picturesque organization of house clusters around a common parking lot, while eliminating the danger of individual car entries, makes for odd-shaped lots. Outside spaces are virtually unusable. Functionally this is not very different from the developers' subdivision.

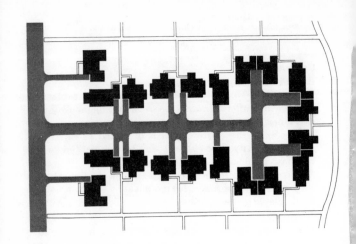

3   *Garden City Organization, Radburn*   *Wright and Stein*
20 houses/cluster   7500 sq. ft./house   6 houses/acre
21 persons/acre

Critique

B   Individual garages, though convenient, disperse vehicle access. There is no provision for temporary off-street parking.

C   Double access from opposite sides of the house makes entry unclear. Entry on the pedestrian side is protected by the patios, but the entry used by visitors and others is on the service side and unprotected.

E   Dispersal and low density keep the noise level down. Pedestrian areas are well screened from service noises. There are no effective noise buffers between the houses themselves and the service and car zone.

F   No special provision has been made for servicing and garbage collection.

G   There is good separation of a vehicular zone from a park zone, but activity in the service area will attract children (where they can best be supervised in any case since the kitchens are on this side of the house). Except for houses on the periphery, protection from urban noise is good.

Conclusion

Radburn is the classic example of early garden-city planning. While accepting the one car per family pattern of American life, it tries to separate vehicles and pedestrians. The generous provision of communal park space raises new problems of ownership and responsibility.

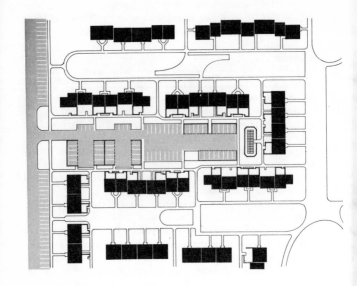

4   *Garden City Cluster Organization, Baldwin Hills   Wright and Stein*
30 houses/cluster   5400 sq. ft./house   8 houses/acre
28 persons/acre

Critique

B   Parking is well organized except for a few possible bottle-necks. Pedestrian access points are widely scattered and make for lack of control.

C   Entrance from parking is visually and acoustically protected by the private court. Entry from the pedestrian side exposed to all local interference.

E   Private courts form a buffer between vehicles and dwellings, but neighbor noises are uncontrolled and likely to prove a nuisance.

F   Servicing and garbage collection dominate the parking area when they occur.

G   Although the shape and location of the parking lot mini-mizes walking distance between house and car, it makes control of children impossible. The position of the child-lot aggravates this fault. Pedestrian-vehicle separation is good. Except for those on the periphery, houses are buffered from urban noise.

Conclusion

An improved version of the original Radburn principle, by the same planners. Car accommodation has been extended and consolidated. There is a buffer zone between the vehicles and the dwellings. The outdoor space has been more pre-cisely allocated to pleasure and use. The plan is extravagant in communal garden space at the expense of private out-door space.

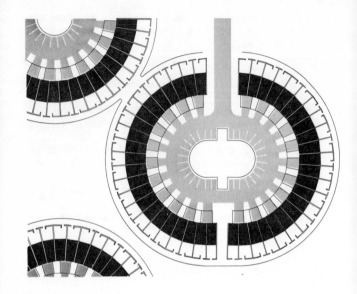

5 *Garden City Cluster Organization, Eastwick   Greentown Associates*
44 houses/cluster   5000 sq. ft./house   9 houses/acre
32 persons/acre

Critique

B   There is no transfer zone. The central area contains both off-street and street parking. Pedestrians cross the service street to reach their cars.

C   Entries, though partially screened, are visible from nearly all the other dwellings because of the circular arrangement.

E   The communal outdoor space is buffered from the traffic noise by the dwellings themselves. The dwellings are buffered from communal noise by the private courts. The acoustic advantage to rooms on the outside are offset inside by the court shape, the worst possible choice; it will contain all local noises and transmit them to every dwelling.

F   Service and garbage collection take place in the focus of communal activity.

G   Some parts of the communal area are separated from vehicles. Since all the outdoor spaces leak into one another, separation is not consistently maintained, which makes it unusable for children and animals.

Conclusion

A "bull ring"; the parking lot is framed by the entries and bedrooms of attached row houses. The use of the parking lot and service street as a *focus* for a residential cluster is highly questionable. The form of the clusters makes the pedestrian outdoor realm a shapeless leftover. There is no logical place for community structures and much waste space.

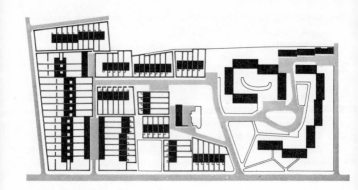

6 *Modified Garden City Organization, Blackheath, London Eric Lyons*
76 houses/cluster   4500 sq. ft./house   10 houses/acre
34 persons/acre

Critique

B Apartment parking and lock-up gates are dispersed. There is only unplanned car storage, and no transfer zone.

C Entry to court houses is well protected. Other dwelling types have entries which are difficult to control visually and acoustically.

E No attempt has been made to control noise produced either inside or outside the community.

F Servicing will cause just as much interference as it does in existing street systems.

G Vehicles and pedestrians are not separated. Many peripheral dwellings are not protected from traffic noise.

Conclusion

The plan is a mixture of dwelling styles for a medium-high density area. The parking area is underestimated, and confused with the inner pedestrian realm. A tidy, charming "stage set" that ignores many realities of its day.

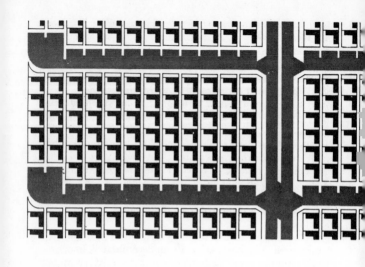

7 *The "Logical" Diagram, A new settlement unit*   *Hilberseimer*
70 houses/cluster   3200 sq. ft./house   14 houses/acre
50 persons/acre

Critique

C Dwelling entries are visually private; but there is serious conflict between the noise and activity generated in narrow
walled passages that will disturb the master bedroom of the
next house which is immediately opposite.

E The communal domains are separated from the dwellings;
they cannot be reached without crossing traffic. Reduction
of noise from house to house is well provided for by consistent
plan and orientation. The single outdoor space will create
constant conflicts within each family. The boundaries between various realms are well defined.

F Servicing and garbage collection are uncontrolled, and will
therefore tend to disrupt normal street and passage use.

G The fingers of the "dead-end" road plan serve too many
dwellings, so that traffic is itself unnecessarily intensified.
Traffic is not clearly separate from pedestrians. There are
special dangers for children. Garages buffer the dwellings
from traffic noise on only one side of the cluster.

Conclusion

None of the stages in the development of this theoretically
correct organization has provided any humanizing elements
of variety or interest. All the deadly monotonous characteristics of the grid subdivision are heightened.

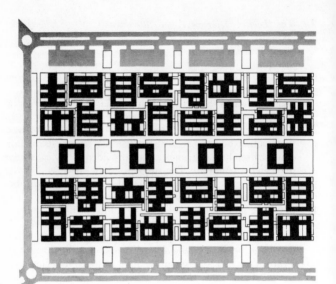

Holzbauer, Arbeitsgruppe 3/4

23 houses/cluster   3000 sq. ft./house   14 houses/acre
51 persons/acre

Critique

B   Parking is well organized as a transition zone between traffic and pedestrians. Parking for each group of four clusters is independent of other circulation, and provides shelter and accommodation.

C   Entries to dwellings are well protected. Enclosure and fragmentation of communal spaces helps to control them visually and acoustically.

F   Public utilities and management service are provided for each cluster of four groups. Garbage could be contained in the service structures.

G   Spaces ideal for communal rest and small children's play are provided at the intersection of pedestrian walks in each cluster. Pedestrians are clearly separated from vehicles. Car-to-dwelling distances are relatively large; but trolleys stored in service structures could overcome this disadvantage. Dwellings on the outside are not protected from urban noise.

Conclusion

A linear plan between highways with parallel parking for clusters of various dwelling types. A park between the dwelling cluster contains kindergarten playgrounds, old-age homes, etc., (which require only intermittent vehicular servicing). The pedestrian circulation system permits a considerable variety of spaces, including nuclei of communal focus. Total use of space. A plan also developed for Vienna by Dr. Roland Reiner, contains many similar features.

9 *Urban Cluster* *Boston Chapter of the CIAM*
35 houses/cluster   4000 sq. ft./house   11 houses/acre
39 persons/acre
Critique

B Parking is adequate; a service truck could probably be accommodated. Good reception vestibule to group, with sheltered facilities. Fire truck can get within easy hose length.

C Entries are well protected, if outdoor vestibule is walled in. Noise from one entry to another would be impossible to control where entries face one another.

E Shelter in vestibule could contain utility controls. Clear boundaries could be established by careful group planning. Houses flanking parking or the service street are not buffered from communal noise.

F Garbage collection would go through pedestrian alleys, and no point for disposal is indicated. Random house distribution complicates layout of utilities.

G Varying rest and play spaces can be provided on park side. Pedestrian-vehicle separation could be provided. Dwelling-to-car distance is short.

Conclusion

A cluster of two-floor prefabricated houses, planned as a flexible yet modular unit for a large sector. Communal parking space and pedestrian "vestibule," which would have to be walled-in to be effective. Houses are approached by pleasant pedestrian alleys. Houses flanking parking are at a disadvantage. The private outdoor spaces would be exposed to neighbors.

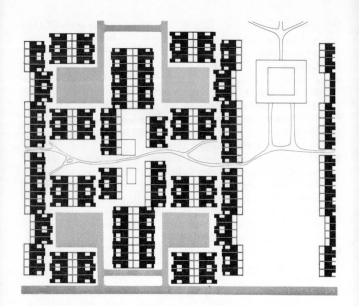

Joseph Zalewski

44 houses/cluster   4000 sq. ft./house   11 houses/acre
39 persons/acre

Critique

B   There is enough parking and maneuver space for all vehicles. There is ample transition from highway traffic. There is no central reception point. Each group is focused on the cars and service.

C   Nearly half the entries are very public and open to the parking court. This parking court will make it difficult to shield entries from local noise.

E   There are no special service spaces. Access to clusters cannot be barred. Boundaries are clear. Small interior courts are good acoustically. Parking courts will generate and aggravate local noise.

F   Garbage collection and servicing will disturb all houses on the parking court.

G   The relatively dense building coverage will reduce general urban noise. Pleasant rest and play areas can be provided along the mall. Children and pets cannot be kept away from traffic. Distances from dwelling to car are short.

Conclusion

The pedestrian walks and community spaces form a grid to complement the traffic pattern and link to form a continuous pedestrian mall. Car parking is peripheral. The character of the pedestrian outdoor spaces is so similar to the parking courts that children most likely will spill from one to the other.

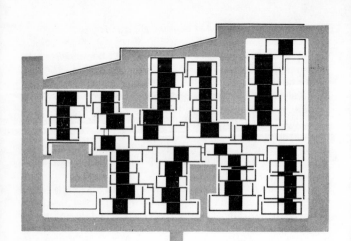

11 *Urban Renewal Group, Yale School of Architecture*   D. E. R. Scott
44 houses/cluster   5000 sq. ft./house   10 houses/acre
36 persons/acre

Critique

B Parking occurs between existing street and a pedestrian realm, with ample space for other vehicles. There is no sheltered reception point, but this could be provided.

C Privacy of entry is protected by patios, except where two-floor houses overlook them.

E Access points could be barred. There are clear boundaries. The high density and position of the patios buffer the houses against urban noise.

F Garbage collection and services could be relegated to the periphery.

G Pedestrians are well separated from vehicles, access to the communal domain being solely through clearly articulated entrances. No attempt has been made to buffer the dwellings abutting the highways from urban noise.

Conclusion

The project applies a system of clusters to an existing renewal site, omitting community structures which might, however, be included. Parking is peripheral and pedestrian movement central on a spine and rib plan.

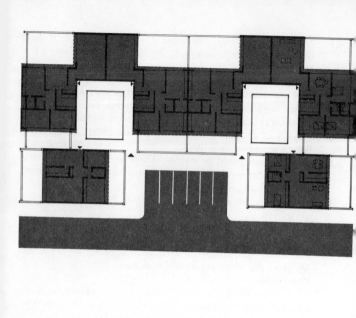

12   *Urban Cluster, Yale School of Architecture Thesis*   *Kozinsky*
         6 houses/cluster   3600 sq. ft./house   12 houses/acre
         42 persons/acre

Critique

B   Parking needs more transition space. Sheltered reception
         point could be provided.

C   Small courts protect the house entries, though they might
         generate annoying noise.

E   No consolidated garbage or service point for the cluster.
         Access to courts can be barred. There are clear boundaries.
         Fragmented walled open spaces will reduce urban noise.
         The bedroom courts of the four houses that flank the parking
         area are at a disadvantage.

F   Garbage collection is not provided for.

G   This cluster alone is too small to provide rest or play spaces,
         unless inner courts are so used. Buffer from urban noise could
         be provided. Dwelling-to-car distance is minimal.

Conclusion

A self-contained efficient modular cluster of six one-floor
houses for a small site. The number of houses makes communal facilities impractical unless this cluster is a cell in a
larger group. Additional parking and service must be provided on the access street.

13 *Urban Cluster*

Alexander, Meunier, P. Chermayeff, Reynolds, Christie

20 houses/cluster   3100 sq. ft./house   14 houses/acre
51 persons/acre

Critique

B Parking off a one-way system: special truck drawoff. Sheltered reception point. Controlled transition into one-way traffic. Emergency access through parking lot.

C All entries are buffered by courts. Entry is sheltered. Organization is such that no entry is opposite another, giving maximum privacy. Pedestrian alleys minimize noise that can be generated by entry.

E Utility and service structure is a separate entity. Boundaries are clear. Access points can be barred. Fragmentation of space gives optimum acoustic condition in private outdoor spaces. Noise is further dispersed by diluting pedestrian circulation.

F Garbage collection point is enclosed and isolated. Utilities are centrally controlled and arranged on a grid accessible in the alleys.

G Variety of interior rest and play spaces are available off the alleys where there are no entries. There is total separation of children and pets from vehicles. Distance from inner dwellings to car is somewhat long, but this disadvantage can be overcome by trolleys stored and operated from the central reception point provided. Each cluster of one-floor court dwellings and alleys is a walled realm, tending to reduce urban noise.

Conclusion

This plan is a translation of our analytical diagrams into a cluster that could be incorporated in a linear or superblock sector plan with highway access or in smaller units with one-way service road access. A complete pedestrian walk-way system links all units. Community and service structures form a barrier between vehicles and pedestrians and a focus for community activity.

13

ANATOMY OF PRIVACY

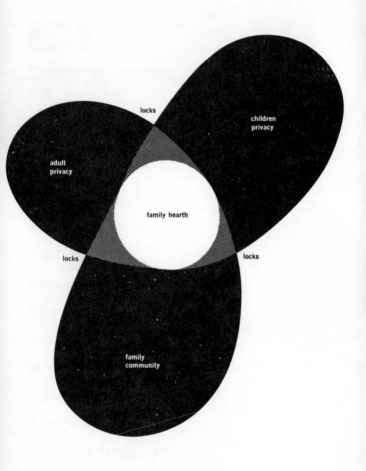

Anatomy of Dwelling: people

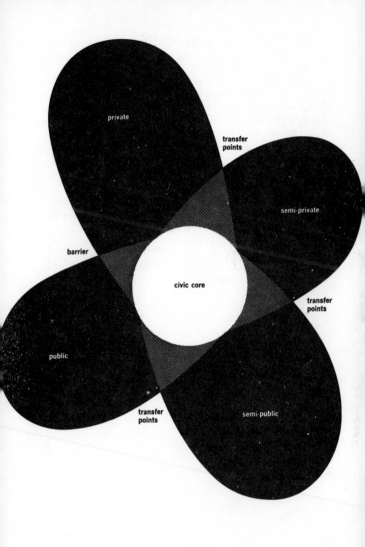

Anatomy Of Urban Realms: areas of responsibility

Good design means going back to fundamentals: a child at work in a stable and reassuring world: a pair of lovers at play in a room where the scent of lilacs may creep through the window, or the shrill piping of crickets be heard in the garden below.

. . . the child is no less entitled to space, room for play and movement, a place for quiet retreat and study, other than his bed. No housing standard is adequate that provides only cubicles or dressing rooms for the child, or forces him into the constant company of adults.

Lewis Mumford
The Culture of Cities, 1938

"Dadda! I wanna come in!"

"Well, you can't. Clear out!"

"But dadda! I wanna go somewhere!"

"Go somewhere else, then. Hop it. I'm having my bath."

"Dad-da! I wanna go somewhere!"

No use! I knew the danger signal. The w.c. is in the bathroom . . . it would be, of course, in a house like ours. I hooked the plug out of the bath and got partially dry as quickly as I could.

George Orwell
Coming Up for Air, 1939

Hierarchies of Joints

Irrespective of their function and size, the diverse domains of the modern world are multiplying and are susceptible to rapid change and to a variety of conflicts between them. These domains can not only be abstractly explained in terms of function or need but can be precisely described in terms of physical properties which may be directly perceived. The conflicts between these properties can be very real and sharply drawn. The integrity of each space, the preservation of its special, carefully specified environmental characteristics, depends on the physical elements that provide separation, insulation, access, and controlled transfer between domains.

We have discussed the hierarchy of domains. Once one realizes that the joints between domains are themselves physical elements of no less importance, one can see that it is actually these elements that give the plan its hierarchical structure.

Vehicles and pedestrians need strict separation; neighboring houses need insulation against fire and noise and other external factors; and the skin of the dwelling needs to separate the inside from a hostile climate. Barriers, modulators, and similar devices, permanent or temporary, must be provided to screen living creatures, light, and sounds; to separate the desirable from the undesirable. The appropriate separating device works in the manner of a joint. In fact, the most important lesson to be learned from our detailed analysis is that each different joint has its own special form. Terms like baffle, barrier, buffer, screen, filter, transfer point, lock, junction, terminal, serve to distinguish them roughly. But though they form a family of a sort, in the last analysis each is different and specific to its individual position in the hierarchy.

It is essential to avoid the trap of thinking that the particular results of our analysis are valid at all scales of the urban form. Only the general principle is universal.

Anatomy of Dwelling

The individual dwelling plan we are looking for must have special components, analogous to those of the dwelling clusters previously analyzed. Before we can specify them at this scale, we must describe the attributes our commitment to privacy and community demands, and the domains that will accommodate them within the dwelling.

The Outdoor Room

The dwelling, if it is for a family, must be in immediate contact with nature. Since this dwelling is to be composed of a series of carefully organized realms, each with its own integrity, each indoor realm must have its own concomitant outdoor space. Just as there must be a hierarchy of man-made domains in the city, so, too, the enjoyment of nature demands its own hierarchy of scale and subdivision, ranging from the great natural landscape to the tiny cultivated outdoor room of one's own.

Secondly, every dwelling must contain an acoustic hierarchy, closely linked to the enjoyment of sun, air, and light, so that even in the outdoor room of one's own, the smallest desired sound can be heard and enjoyed.

A Room of One's Own

The integrity of domestic domains, which is to encourage concentration, contemplation, and self-reliance rather than inhibit them, must begin by respecting differences in age, sex, and interest. In particular, the integrity suggested by the word "bedroom," its meaning as a realm of solitude, for rest, sleep, and love, must be restored. It seems obvious that this desirable result will be more readily achieved if some of the commonplace facilities now found in the bedroom were removed: storage for personal possessions, facilities for washing, dressing and undressing, primping, *et al.* The lock or buffer zone necessary between the private world and the world of the family can accommodate all of these.

A Family Hearth

Provision for voluntary communality rather than inescapable togetherness is essential. It demands recognition, first of all, of the diversity of interests that occurs in the average family of adults and children; this requires the provision of separate domains in which either group may be left decently to its own devices. The separation can be complemented by a combined work-and-ritual room, perhaps a restoration of the ancient family hearth, a natural mixing valve.

The Service Cores

Proper weight must also be given to the new, almost totally uninhabited areas that are essential parts of contemporary house organization: in a technologically advanced society mechanical controls, storage, utilities, and communications become vital. Certain equipment has already been well organized in the "mechanical cores": food processing and conservation machinery, climatic control mechanisms, and plumbing. Electronic equipment: telephones, radios, TV, hi-fi recordings, film and slide projection remain unorganized.

Climatic Hierarchy

Closer and more exact bodily comfort and cleanliness could follow suit. Both clothes and cars, as suggested previously, are portable shelters. There might well be an increased number of transition points between the relatively uncontrollable or even hostile larger environment and the easily controlled smaller spaces. In the former, the individual must be suitably dressed to meet the demands of social mores as well as climate. In the latter, the same individual in privacy might be as undressed as his taste dictates.

At present civilized overdressed man is confined to the donning and doffing of overcoats, overshoes, and overcars, a crude expedient, leaving him most ineffectively clothed in most situations. Possibly we should shed cars much sooner than we usually do; the severe climatic transition from car to dwelling can be dealt with separately; and cars could be kept at a discreet distance without any loss of comfort.

Outdoor clothes might in their turn be shed at the entrance to the dwelling, thereby leaving external dirt and infection behind before proceeding to the interior, controlled environment, for the enjoyment of which other appropriate private garb might be put on as in the most excellent Japanese tradition.

To fill out the hierarchy of climatic conditions the private realm could be designed in terms of the temperature, humidity, and air movement suitable for naked and near-naked bodies, so that the transition point between private and family domains would also act as a climatic lock between the condition of undress and that designed for more elaborately clothed bodies.

Locks in Action

The idea of locks between different activities as a planning device is not new. In hospitals, contaminated general purpose areas are separated from sterile areas such as operating rooms by sterilization locks through which all persons and equipment must pass. The same principle is employed in broadcasting studios where acoustic locks separate traffic noise from the production areas. Similar, less elaborate locks are a commonplace of modern hotel

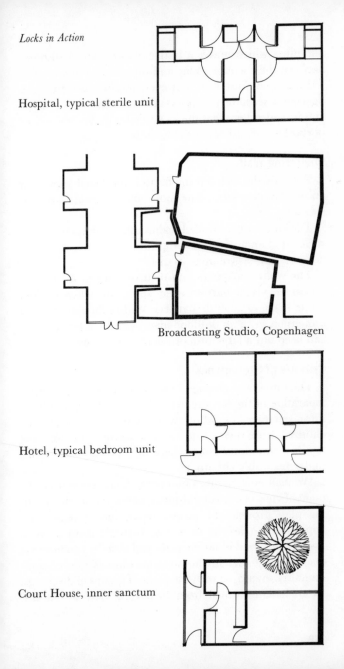

Locks in Action

Hospital, typical sterile unit

Broadcasting Studio, Copenhagen

Hotel, typical bedroom unit

Court House, inner sanctum

planning, which makes a buffer of entry and bathroom between the corridor traffic and the sleeping areas.

In all these instances, however, the lock is virtually a passage: a secondary transition between two major zones. It is intended here that the lock eventually become as important as any other zone of activity.

Sheltering Wall

Not only the lock but the barrier too is well known, in an old familiar form. The most efficient total barrier is *the wall*.

The enclosure for walled realms can be adequately constructed of an ancient material with an infinite variety of faces but all "as common as dirt."

The walls may come into their own again as security measures, visual barriers, and above all, when of adequate mass, as acoustic barriers. Within modest limits of dimension even an outdoor space, when walled around, can keep out a large proportion of external noise.

Critique of Stereotypes

The functional zoning of the house depends on proper separation of the socially defined realms. Walls and locks must separate the adults with their privacy from the children with theirs, and must separate both from the family community zone where mixing may take place under favorable conditions.

We shall now discuss a number of house plans from the point of view of our commitment, namely: does the dwelling plan provide the proper separation of *realms* and appropriate *transitions* or *barriers* between them so as to assure their individual integrity and thereby promote the *enjoyment of privacy* in the same measure as that of communality. Again, as with the plans of groups of dwellings, we are looking at them from the point of view of organization; we are not looking for structural or mechanical specifications or aesthetic values.

The house plans selected for analysis here are representative examples of "well-designed" houses. They can be conveniently grouped as follows:

Rural-suburban Single Family Houses. Standing free in their own "grounds." Ranging from the small lot giving relatively low density "own ground" in name only to substantial land area per house and density actually low enough to make some separation between houses possible.

Urban-suburban Attached Houses. Compact small houses of one or more floors with generous front and back "yards" to each; these *row* houses of minimal road frontage share "party" walls, and are designed for relatively high densities.

Urban Attached Houses. Varying in accommodation, land coverage, and grouping, the compact plans are designed for high densities. Each house is provided with private outdoor space.

The examples included in the above categories were preselected by their publication in the architectural press. All the designs are of high quality in the conventional architectural sense. Our critique is of course concerned with other criteria that derive from our commitment to problems of privacy and community. Therefore our critique will be confined to an examination of the effectiveness of each plan from this point of view.

To simplify the critical appraisal and to make this analogous to the detailed cluster analysis, the following questions are asked in each instance.

1   Is there an entry "lock" to give the house as a whole an adequate buffer zone against intrusion? Question of protection.

2   Is the children's domain directly accessible from outside so as not to interfere with the adult's private and

family domains? Questions of noise, interruption, and "dirt."

3 Is there a buffer zone between the children's private domain and the parents' private domain? Question of noise.

4 Is there a "lock" to the parents' private domain? Questions of noise, interruption, and modesty.

5 Can a "living room" be isolated acoustically, as either a quiet or a noisy zone, from the rest of the house? Questions of separating sounds of conversation, "listening" and "looking," from silent occupations such as reading.

6 Are the outdoor spaces private and differentiated? Questions of interference between children's and adults', and between individual and family, domains.

In addition to the more conventional plans described above, some prototype plans still under development, which are attempts to meet our criteria, are also included:

Urban Attached Court Houses. Single floor houses of varying accommodation but all planned as "walled realms" that are zoned in distinct domains: adults' and children's privacy, and family community. Each domain has its own outdoor space. All are designed for high densities and grouping in clusters within a pedestrian realm.

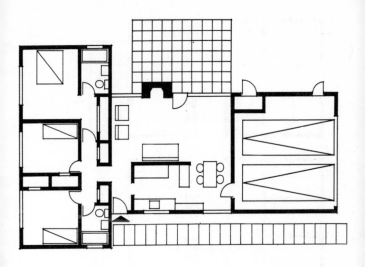

1 *Houses in California on 50′ lots*   *Jones and Emmons*

Critique

1 Entry lock to house   **No**
2 Separate children's   **Yes**
   access
3 Buffer, parents/   **No**
   children
4 Lock to parents'   **Yes**
   bedroom
5 Can living room be   **No**
   isolated
6 Are outdoor spaces   **No**
   private

Conclusion

The houses, oriented toward neighbors on both sides, are far too close together for proper private use of outdoor spaces. This failure is all the more conspicuous in the context of the California climate that favors outdoor living. Planting can only provide visual barriers; it has no effect on noise.

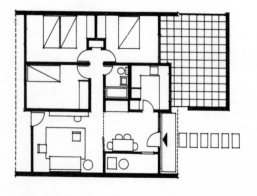

2 *Family House, Techbuilt Homes, Inc.*　　　　*Carl Koch*

Critique

1	Entry lock to house	**No**	
2	Separate children's access	**Yes**	Could also be provided through multipurpose area.
3	Buffer, parents/children	**No**	All traffic must pass through either living or multipurpose room.
4	Lock to parents' bedroom	**No**	
5	Can living room be isolated	**No**	
6	Are outdoor spaces private	**Yes**	In a modest way. Only the balcony can be considered part of parents' domain.

Conclusion

This is a characteristic "open" plan, providing pleasant-looking spaces. Visual privacy is difficult and acoustic privacy impossible to obtain. The open stair and split-level entry aggravate this condition.

3 *Row House*　　　　*Hugh Stubbins*

Critique

1	Entry lock to house	**No**	
2	Separate children's access	**No**	Children must cross dining and living areas.
3	Buffer, parents/children		Storage wall helps, but all bedrooms open onto a very restricted space; traffic and acoustic chaos.
4	Lock to parents' bedroom	**No**	
5	Can living room be isolated	**No**	There is no quiet room.
6	Are outdoor spaces private	**No**	Each outdoor space is in conflict between two functions.

Conclusion

Privacy and quiet are impossible to achieve in this house.

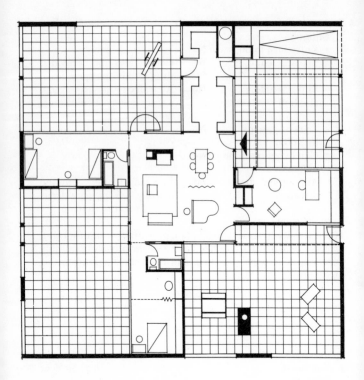

4 *House in California*   *Donald Olsen*

Critique

1 Entry lock to house	**No**	At none of the four entries.
2 Separate children's access	**No**	Children must pass through major living area.
3 Buffer, parents/ children		Adults' sun court acts as buffer but has no visual privacy. Family room acts as buffer when not in use.
4 Lock to parents' bedroom	**No**	A sliding door is inadequate. Another door on the other side of the bathroom would complete the lock.
5 Can living room be isolated	**No**	It is a crossroads. The workroom could have been a quiet room but it is trapped between entries.
6 Are outdoor spaces private	**Yes**	Well zoned, all could be made private.

Conclusion

In spite of all the adverse criticisms this plan shows the germs of a very adequate solution. The absence of any programmatic demand for privacy has prevented zoning of activities from being carried through.

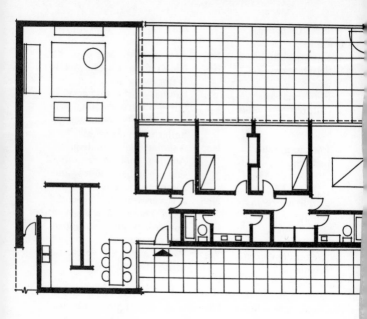

5 *Court Houses, Michigan*   *Mies van der Rohe*

Critique

1	Entry lock to house	**Yes**	But entry is exposed.
2	Separate children's access	**Yes**	
3	Buffer, parents/ children	**No**	Passage contains all traffic. Only a partition wall separates children and parents. The shared court prevents both visual and acoustic privacy.
4	Lock to parents' bedroom	**Yes**	
5	Can living room be isolated	**No**	The dining area, if considered the active room, is inadequately separated.
6	Are outdoor spaces private	**No**	The single court conflicts with private realms.

Conclusion

The single court together with the open plan of the living and service wing cancels out many possible advantages of this plan.

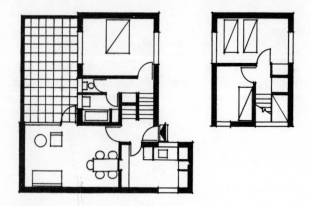

6 *Court Houses, London*　　　　*Chamberlain, Powell, and Bon*
Critique

1	Entry lock to house	**Yes**	
2	Separate children's access	**Yes**	
3	Buffer, parents/ children	**Yes**	Two flights of stairs. But visual privacy of parents' bedroom is easily violated from common court.
4	Lock to parents' bedroom		Two doors from living room, kitchen, and children's bedrooms, but shared bathroom is a limitation.
5	Can living room be isolated	**No**	No quiet room.
6	Are outdoor spaces private	**No**	The single inside court, without any other outdoor space, invites conflict between parents' and family domains.

Conclusion

A great deal has been sacrificed for economy. Parents' bedroom has been isolated as much as possible but shared bathroom negates the good arrangement.

7 *Terrace Housing, Blackheath, London*   *Eric Lyons*
Critique

1	Entry lock to house	**Yes**	Yes
2	Separate children's access	**Yes**	Stairs open to entry lock and proceed behind doors directly to bedrooms.
3	Buffer, parents/children	**No**	
4	Lock to parents' bedroom	**No**	
5	Can living room be isolated	**Yes**	But study should be protected from noisy family activities.
6	Are outdoor spaces private	**No**	Entry court is public.

Conclusion

The plan is partially successful within very restricted dimensions but invites much dangerous stair traffic. There is no outdoor space for children.

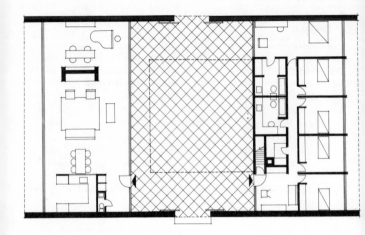

Critique

1 Entry lock to house   **Yes**
2 Separate children's   **Yes**
  access
3 Buffer, parents/   **No**
  children
4 Lock to parents'   **No**
  bedroom
5 Can living room be
  isolated

> In common with many plans the study here is a space put apart from the major living area by a partial barrier, in this case a large fireplace. As this house was designed by the architect for himself we can only conclude that he has opted for partial community rather than strict privacy.

6 Are outdoor spaces   **No**
  private

Conclusion

The house is split into two zones, the formal entry court forming the buffer reinforced by the bath and storage rooms. Complete solitude and privacy would be difficult to achieve without considerable rearrangement.

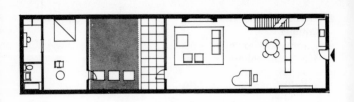

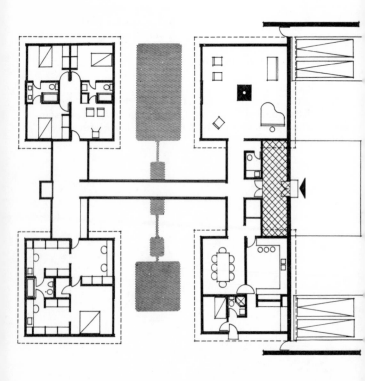

9 *Row House, Rockefeller Guest House, N.Y.*   *Philip Johnson*
   Critique

1 Entry lock to house	**Yes**	Inferred but not complete.
2 Separate children's access	**Yes**	If upstairs accommodation becomes children's domain.
3 Buffer, parents/children	**Yes**	Entire ground floor area forms buffer.
4 Lock to parents' bedroom	**Yes**	Interior court acts as lock.
5 Can living room be isolated	**No**	
6 Are outdoor spaces private	**Yes**	Court may be shut off from either bedroom or sitting room.

   Conclusion

This house designed for guests could work well as a family house. There is a hierarchy of increasing privacy as one penetrates deeper.

10 *House in Louisiana*   *Colbert and Lowry*
   Critique

1 Entry lock to house	**Yes**	
2 Separate children's access	**Yes**	
3 Buffer, parents/children	**Yes**	
4 Lock to parents' bedroom	**Yes**	
5 Can living room be isolated	**Yes**	Study and television rooms in two bedroom wings are well buffered from other activities.
6 Are outdoor spaces private	**Yes**	With additional walls.

   Conclusion

Solitude, privacy, and quiet are easy to obtain in this well-zoned house with an unusual amount of ground coverage and expanse.

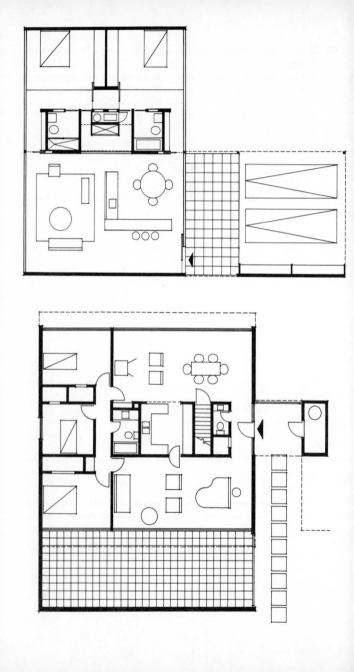

11 *House in California*   *Pierre Koenig*
   Critique
   1 Entry lock to house   **No**   But could be provided.
   2 Separate children's   **No**   Children must pass through
      access   living room.
   3 Buffer, parents/   **Yes**
      children
   4 Lock to parents'   Could easily be provided for
      bedroom   both bedrooms.
   5 Can living room be   **No**
      isolated
   6 Are outdoor spaces   Only if main bedroom and
      private   living room are taken to be
                                        in one zone.
   Conclusion
   The duplication of facilities (bed and bath) allows good zoning
   and permits a clear system of locks.

12 *House in Michigan*   *Meathe and Kessler*
   Critique
   1 Entry lock to house   **Yes**
   2 Separate children's   **Yes** Through family room.
      access
   3 Buffer, parents/   **No**   But there could be.
      children
   4 Lock to parents'   **No**   But there could be.
      bedroom
   5 Can living room be   **Yes**
      isolated
   6 Are outdoor spaces   **Yes**
      private
   Conclusion
   A clear bizonal plan, with a continuous spine of buffer and lock
   between adults and children, between family and guests.

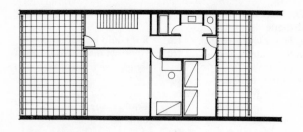

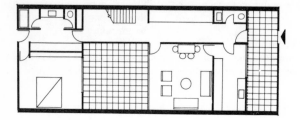

13 *Two Story Row House for a Cluster*   *Barry Coletti and Chermayeff*

Critique

1	Entry lock to house	**Yes**	The addition of a door would further isolate entry from central circulation space.
2	Separate children's access	**No**	Difficult in a two story plan.
3	Buffer, parents/ children	**Yes**	Central court and change of level.
4	Lock to parents' bedroom	**Yes**	
5	Can living room be isolated	**Yes**	Children have private roof decks, but there is no separate family room.
6	Are outdoor spaces private	**Yes**	But partial use by children of the living-dining room forces a partial sharing of the central court with the main bedroom.

Conclusion

Adults' and children's domains are separated three dimensionally in this house and well provided with dressing and hygiene locks. The combination living-family room, however, invites children's use of the central court and reduces the privacy of the adult domain.

14 *Court House for a Cluster*　　　　*Frank Sweet and Chermayeff*
Critique
1	Entry lock to house	**Yes**	A double lock.
2	Separate children's access	**Yes**	Through children's court.
3	Buffer, parents/children	**Yes**	The family room and court.
4	Lock to parents' bedroom	**Yes**	
5	Can living room be isolated	**Yes**	
6	Are outdoor spaces private		Only partially. Two bedrooms, including the master bedroom, share the central court with the kitchen-dining room. The end court is shared by a family room and a children's bedroom.

Conclusion

The house is divided into two clear realms for adults and children, each protected by effective locks. The central family area including kitchen and dining acts as a buffer between the living room and the children's room. The two bedrooms opening onto the family court are a serious weakness.

15 *Court House for a Cluster* *Chermayeff*

Critique

1	Entry lock to house	**Yes**	
2	Separate children's access	**Yes**	Through children's court.
3	Buffer, parents/children	**Yes**	The family room and court.
4	Lock to parents' bedroom	**Yes**	
5	Can living room be isolated	**Yes**	
6	Are outdoor spaces private	**Yes**	Each of four zones have their own outdoor extension; parents' bedroom, living room, family room, and children's rooms.

Conclusion

The family room containing all food preparation in its logical central position makes a three-zone plan possible. The bedroom-study opening onto the family court is at a disadvantage.

16 *Court House for a Cluster* *Robert Gordon and Chermayeff*

Critique

1	Entry lock to house	**Yes**	
2	Separate children's access	**Yes**	Through children's court.
3	Buffer, parents/children	**Yes**	Service core and court.
4	Lock to parents' bedroom	**Yes**	Dressing room in service spine.
5	Can living room be isolated	**Yes**	
6	Are outdoor spaces private	**Yes**	Living room has two courts which can act as buffer zones as well.

Conclusion

This larger area plan has six interior patios on two sides of a service spine, which enables the zoning to fall into four clear zones; adults, family, parents and guests, and children. The guest room-study opening onto the family court is at the same disadvantage as the above plan.

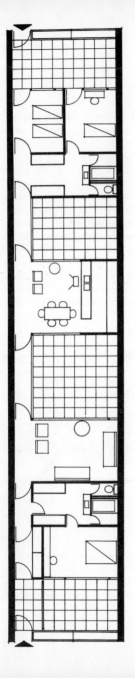

children

family

adults

17 *Court House, Harvard*   *Robert Reynolds and Chermayeff*

Critique

1	Entry lock to house	**Yes**	Walled outdoor court and entry hall.
2	Separate children's access	**Yes**	Through both or either of children's rooms.
3	Buffer, parents/children	**Yes**	Hygiene and dressing areas buffer parents' bedroom. Dining room and court form buffer between family and sitting rooms. Entire length of house forms buffer between parents' private realm and children's private realm.
4	Lock to parents' bedroom	**Yes**	All bedrooms are planned as bed-sitting rooms with locks of hygiene and dressing.
5	Can living room be isolated	**Yes**	Either as a smaller separate zone or by entering the family room from the direction of the children's end of the house.
6	Are outdoor spaces private	**Yes**	With sufficient lot depth to add an outside court in the children's realm three totally separate outdoor zones are obtainable: adult. family, children.

Conclusion

In spite of very narrow frontage the plan gives good separation of domains acoustically. The central family realm makes a good buffer between adults and children, and each private realm is buffered by a dressing-hygiene lock.

14

NEW PLANNING BLOCKS

Community and Privacy

Barriers and Locks

Hierarchical Organization

Hierarchy of Conservation

The Innermost Sanctum

Art and Science

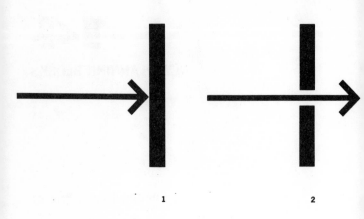

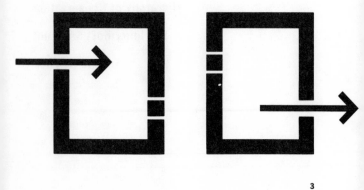

Diagram of sequence of development from the *barrier* to the *lock*

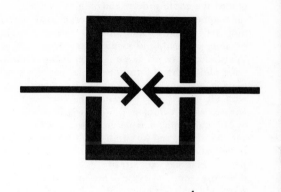

4

5

Yet if the continuity of pattern is valid there must exist scientific principles of form and structure which have guided the entire process and must appear, though possibly disguised, in many realms, inorganic, personal, and social. We can look forward to a unifying philosophy of form, displaying wherein we are one with all nature and wherein we are uniquely human.

This philosophy may not lie very far ahead, and its formulation may be eased by anticipation. For one can already recognize some rules which seem to be widely, though perhaps not universally, applicable. Since at this stage they can only be expressed vaguely, without specifying the exact conditions under which they are valid, they are certainly not yet scientific. But they may be on the way to it. . . .

Lancelot Law Whyte
Invisible Structure
Accent on Form: An Anticipation of the Science of Tomorrow, 1954

Only the free-wheeling artist-explorer, non-academic scientist philosopher, mechanic, economist poet who has never waited for patron-startering and accrediting of his coordinate capabilities holds the prime initiative today. If man is to continue as a successful pattern-complex function in universal evolution, it will be because the next decades will have witnessed the artist-scientist's spontaneous seizure of the prime design responsibility and his successful conversion of the total capability of tool-augmented man from killingry to livingry.

R. Buckminster Fuller
Prime Design
Arts and Architecture, September 1962

NEW PLANNING BLOCKS

Community and Privacy

We have chosen to look at a tiny part of the urban form and have scrutinized it in rather fine detail from the point of view of *community* and *privacy*. As a result of this inquiry certain issues have dug themselves deeper and deeper into the bones of the inquiry, and a special attitude toward all urban forms has been generated. Not only the cluster of dwellings and the house itself need to contain barriers and locks. The diagrams opening this chapter apply at every scale in the urban hierarchy. The integrity of domains and the efficiency of transfer between them is the crucial issue in organization.

Barriers and Locks

Who and what interferes with what and whom, to what extent, when and how, are significant questions that the urban designer now has to ask himself. The condition where the integrity of each of the adjoining domains must be preserved at all times, in spite of traffic between them, immediately brings to mind the familiar canal lock which separates two different water levels, or the air lock which allows movement between areas of different air pressure. We can easily see our analogous social, visual, acoustic, climatic, and technical purposes in the same terms. Each kind of integrity can be maintained only by its particular locks and buffer zones.

Thus the results of a limited but typical inquiry has served as a jumping-off point for a whole series of ideas about man-made environments. A general planning principle inherent in the structure of a whole class of problems has been exposed. The *transition points* that at first appeared as secondary joints between realms now emerge as important primary elements in their own right. They are fully fledged and vital physical entities, crucial planning

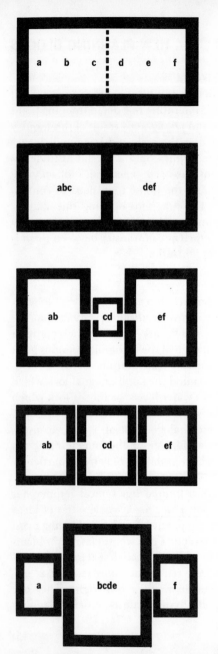

The *lock* emerges as a *realm* and *activity zone*.

elements suited to a mobile, mechanized, and noisy world.

By organizing our commitment to restore equilibrium between community and privacy, we have identified and formulated these physical joints to the extent where they can serve as new practical blocks for planners—building blocks that may be put to immediate use.

Hierarchical Organization

More important, we have suggested that behind the principle of articulate and efficient jointing systems it is possible to recognize a diversity of hierarchies of organization—hierarchies diverse in their function and form, yet intricately and intimately interwoven in their effect on planning concepts and physical form.

Within each hierarchical order one may perceive a far greater spectrum of scale than appeared at first sight. It is not only the man-made that is susceptible to hierarchical organization employing to the limit knowledge, technology, and art. The imminent destruction of the natural requires the application of the same principle to programs of conservation.

Hierarchy of Conservation

The mechanized comforts and conveniences one can now enjoy are leaving great scars in the natural environment which one could otherwise also enjoy. At present few people hesitate to cut down an ancient great tree to make room for a trivial, short-lived house which should, in fact, accommodate itself to antiquity and grandeur. Perhaps we need laws to protect great trees from private vandalism by making them part of the public realm. The dramatic dimensions of national park and seashore preservation measures tend to divert us from the continuing erosion of nature on our doorsteps.

In his declining years Edward Steichen, the photographer, has been recording, day by day, the effects of seasons, weather, and light on the shadbush outside his window. In the words of René d'Harnoncourt, he has transformed it into a "tree of life." So, from the smallest outdoor space within the urban environment, either predominantly natural or artificial, one could construct an imaginative hierarchical order through the whole spectrum of the enjoyment of nature reaching out toward the largest wilderness.

The Innermost Sanctum

We have suggested above all else that the various hierarchies of organization of the human habitat should be extended toward the neglected realm of the private: the innermost sanctum, the room of one's own, indoor and outdoor, to balance the places of domestic and civic scale, the cityscape, and the great systems and events to be encountered in the open earth and sky in the company of other people.

Within this great hierarchy of natural and man-made order would be clearly comprehended functions and articulate forms possessed of integrity, nobility, and beauty. To create a better human habitat, both the natural and the man-made must command equal respect.

The hour is late. The validity of any planning principle for conservation or the creation of a human habitat can in the end be proven only in use. For planning ideas to be tested, plans must be executed. A commitment to a system of organization must first be made, and then houses, cities, or perhaps something yet unimagined must be constructed and later inhabited to prove their worth or failure.

Art and Science

Our purpose in this book has been twofold. First, to find a principle of organization that will create a physical environment in which urban man may once more find his life in equilibrium; second, to enable designers so to organize their task that artistic intuition and technical capacity can work together.

At present, art and science appear to be wandering their separate ways like parted lovers who, in search of solace, take refuge in promiscuity. Civilized man must give high priority to the development of a unified field of environmental control in which art will once again be tempered by the purposeful discipline of science, and science be inspired by the insights of art.

This amalgam could produce a comprehensive design that would not only accommodate Community and Privacy but would celebrate both in the Architecture of a New Humanism.

Art:

Serge Chermayeff   Christopher Alexander

"In a carefully studied and detailed analysis, Chermayeff and Alexander propose a new kind of urban order, structured to provide clearly-articulated domains within which various human needs can be fulfilled without interference or conflict with other activities. Their hierarchy of spaces and realms extends from the largest aspect of public urban life to the smallest of individual solitude and is designed to create a rational order of physical relationships based on human qualities. . . .

"The merit of their work . . . lies in the breadth of its thesis and the careful detailing of its parts." — Clark P. Turner, *The Humanist*.

". . . the architect-authors are impressively able to practice — in a specific design program — what they so eloquently preach. In the second half of the book, they devote themselves to 'the urban dwelling.' In logically defining its basic requirements, in the context of total environment, and then developing a set of design principles drawn from the interaction of those requirements, they have made a substantial contribution to architectural theory." — Allan Temko, *The New York Times Book Review*.

"This book deserves close study because it analyses human needs and makes them crystal clear." — Jan White, *House and Home*.

"Using a computer to simplify and structure their numerous requirements for a dwelling, the authors have evolved a series of experimental cluster plans that are fascinating in their implications for livability." — Frederick Gutheim, *The Nation*.

DESIGN: PETER CHERMAYEFF

COMMUNITYANDPRIVACY
Toward a New Architecture of Humanism

0-385-03476-8

8-202

A Doubleday   Anchor Book